Advance Praise
The Magnanimous Heart

"I loved this book—and I felt inspired, held, and perfectly guided by it. We need this kind of honest teaching now, more than ever."
— Norman Fischer, poet and Zen priest, author of *What Is Zen?*

"A beautiful simpatico expression of Narayan's Dharma transmissions in Chan and Vipassana meditation. She handles the subjects of loss and grief with such kindness and wisdom that the reader inevitably sees the potential for their own spiritual awakening within these often-feared states of mind. It is obvious from reading this book that the hallmark of Narayan's own evolution through loss and grief has been the unmistakable joy that holds the vagaries of life and shines through each page. For those willing to listen and apply her wisdom, Narayan proclaims this joy as our birthright and illuminates our path forward."
— Rodney Smith, author of *Touching the Infinite*

"Narayan's exploration of grief and joy is an inspiration. Her personal experience and the wisdom gleaned from it invite you to engage in deep, liberating practice."
— Sharon Salzberg, author of *Real Love*

"A very powerful, practical guide for living our life as our practice. The teachings in this book will work for all who want love, freedom, and peace of mind."
— George Mumford, author of *The Mindful Athlete*

The
Magnanimous
HEART

Compassion & Love,
Loss & Grief, Joy & Liberation

Narayan Helen Liebenson

FOREWORD BY JOSEPH GOLDSTEIN

Wisdom Publications
199 Elm Street
Somerville, MA 02144 USA
wisdompubs.org

Library of Congress Cataloging-in-Publication Data
Names: Liebenson, Narayan Helen, author.
Title: Magnanimous heart: compassion & love, loss & grief, joy & liberation / by Narayan
Helen Liebenson; foreword by Larry Rosenberg.
Description: Boston: Wisdom Publications, [2018] | Includes index. | Identifiers: LCCN
2018009304 (print) | LCCN 2018036054 (ebook) | ISBN 9781614295082 (ebook) |
ISBN 9781614294856 (hardcover: alk. paper)
Subjects: LCSH: Contentment—Religious aspects—Buddhism. | Generosity—Religious
aspects.—Buddhism. | Magnanimity. | Spiritual life—Buddhism.
Classification: LCC BQ4570.C59 (ebook) | LCC BQ4570.C59 L54 2018 (print) |
DDC 294.3/444—dc23
LC record available at https://lccn.loc.gov/2018009304
ISBN 978-1-61429-485-6   ebook ISBN 978-1-61429-508-2

22 21 20 19 18   5 4 3 2 1

Cover design by Nichole Day / Flying Pan Creative / flyingpancreative.com.
Interior design by Greta D. Sibley. Author photo by Peggy Barnes Lenart.
Set in Garamond Premier Pro 12/18.

Wisdom Publications' books are printed on acid-free paper and
meet the guidelines for permanence and durability of the
Production Guidelines for Book Longevity of the Council on Library Resources.

♻ This book was produced with environmental mindfulness.
For more information, please visit wisdompubs.org/wisdom-environment.

Printed in the United States of America.

To Steven Davis and Sarah Doering

To Iris,

I am holding you
in my heart.

Please keep caring
for yourself & your
own dear heart –

Narayan

Contents

Foreword

BY JOSEPH GOLDSTEIN

IN *THE MAGNANIMOUS HEART*, NARAYAN Liebenson explores the age-old human predicament of seeking happiness and joy in a world often filled with loss and grief, disappointment and frustration. Drawing on the classical teachings of the Buddha and her own rich life experience, Narayan guides the reader on a true vision quest—not for otherworldly experience, but for a new way of understanding the great truths of our lives.

As my first Dharma teacher, Anagarika Munindra, would often say, "If you want to understand your mind, sit down and observe it." Of course, this inquiry into our lives need not be limited to "sitting down"—and Narayan illuminates the journey of discovery in all aspects of our lives.

The transformative power of this book lies in the rare combination of great tenderness of feeling, a deeply felt compassion for the suffering of oneself and others, and a profound insight into the causes of that suffering—and the very real possibilities of peace.

In her very clear and straightforward way, Narayan illuminates how difficulties along the spiritual path can be transformed into liberating wisdom. I highly recommend this book to you. It shows how we can move through these challenges with grace and with an ongoing interest in discovering the ultimate nature of freedom.

JOSEPH GOLDSTEIN is the author of *Mindfulness: A Practical Guide to Awakening*, *A Heart Full of Peace*, and numerous other works.

Preface

HAVING TAUGHT IN A CITY Buddhist center for over thirty years, I have been privileged to accompany countless practitioners through their lives. What this means is that I've been able to observe what happens when people value contemplation and practice in a dedicated way over decades. And of course, all along I have been practicing as well, vitally interested in living more wisely and with a greater degree of compassion, passionately interested in the liberated heart.

To teach the Dharma is to be invited into what is most intimate in people's lives—their hopes, fears, and insights—and to offer in return the Buddha's teachings, its methods and principles of practice. This takes place amid ever-changing conditions—ups and downs, gains and losses, and, for all of us at some point, aging, sickness, and death. To be able to offer a path that actually brings the benefits it promises is rewarding beyond estimation.

The promise of the practice as I understand it is twofold, to aspire to a liberating understanding into the causes of suffering and the causes of happiness as well as to make room for the very human anguish that is part of the lives of most people in this world.

And what I know is this: only sitting in meditation is not enough. Only hearing and studying the words of the Buddha are not enough. Only trying to be awake and aware in one's daily life is not enough. All of these practices have to be undertaken *together* in an integrated way. The practice of training the mind, hearing and studying the teachings, and applying them to every arena of one's daily life—whether conditions are wonderful, mundane, or horrific—are all essential components of a liberated life, a life of contemplation.

Meeting life from a meditative perspective, rather than the prevailing cultural view of success and failure, lets us meet the world as a field of learning. From this perspective, the conditions we encounter in our lives invite us to learn what we need to learn, to use this human life wisely.

The invitation always is: how can I practice in the midst of adversity? That is to say, how can I practice in the midst of a life that does not feel quite right, or in the midst of a life that includes lovely conditions yet still feels incomplete, or in situations in which loss is profound, or at times of struggle with painful emotions, with anxiety and isolation, or with troubling world events. Adversity can mean many things.

The ancient teachings of the Buddha are as applicable today as they were when the Buddha was alive. The human psyche does not seem to have changed. We still long for happiness and peace, and we still mistakenly try to find it in externalities. The questions are these:

Where can the heart's longing be fulfilled? How can we view life's pain as a pathway instead of as only an obstacle? Is there a way to understand loss differently than we do? Answering these questions is the purpose of this book.

The following chapters have a natural sequence. They explore first the reality of loss, then look deeply at our reactions and responses to loss, and conclude by holding up a possibility of living a life of joy and liberation. Yet, rather than being like links in a chain, these themes are like threads in a weaving, with the truths of the Buddha's teachings interwoven throughout.

Throughout the rest of this book, I will weave in various components of the practice, beginning by sharing the context of a challenging and painful period in my life. I will share some of the ways in which I endeavored to apply the teachings and engaged in contemplative methods of practice during that time. In this way, I hope to convey some of the potential fruits of a life of meditation and the path that leads to them.

WITH THE GREATEST APPRECIATION TO Nancy Waring who, with sensitive and careful reviewing, supported me with extraordinary patience and expertise. I am also grateful to my sister, Nancy Liebenson-Davis, my niece, Kelsey Liebenson-Morse, and friends including Stephanie Morgan and Barbara Zilber for their wise companionship, critical advice, and ever-kind hearts, and to Josh Bartok for his skillful editing and guidance. I offer appreciation to Bert Seager and Alisa Wolf as well.

I especially want to express my heartfelt gratitude and appreciation to my great Dharma friend and colleague, Larry Rosenberg.

Meeting him and becoming friends over forty years ago has affected my life in incalculable ways, perhaps most profoundly by introducing the Dharma teaching that meditation is a way of life and that every aspect of our lives is our practice. To have received this as my first Dharma teaching paved the way for all that has come after. Out of this grew a shared vision for the center we co-lead, the Cambridge Insight Meditation Center, which emphasizes formal practice as well as meditation in daily life, valuing both depth and breadth.

I offer the deepest bow of respect to my esteemed teachers and to all of the practitioners I have been fortunate to know. Lastly, with enduring love to my beloved Jonathan: my gratitude is boundless.

PART I

Loss

I

A Constant Squeeze

THE WAYS TO SPEAK ABOUT the Buddha's teachings are count-less. Naturally, we teachers tend to teach what has helped us the most throughout our own lives. The path that the Buddha laid out is often described as a shift out of confusion and into clarity, or from uneasiness to peace, or from inner bondage to inner freedom. I see the path of liberation as a movement out of loss and into inner wholeness.

The Buddha said:

> What is born will die,
> what has been gathered will be dispersed,
> what has been accumulated will be exhausted,
> and what has been built up will collapse.

Yes, I know, this view sounds dismal. Fortunately, it isn't the whole picture. It is a partial description of how things are. Nevertheless, hearing what we all know is true, spelled out so starkly, can bring a kind of relief even as, at the same time, it feels daunting. Although on some level we know it is true, our emotions are not always aligned with our intellect. The Buddha began his teaching with this clear understanding of the human condition. Although there is great beauty in this world, there is also suffering, sometimes great suffering. This suffering is called *dukkha* in Pali, the language in which the Buddha's teachings were first written down (around two hundred years after his death, by the way). What is dukkha? It can be translated as "unsatisfactoriness," "fragility," and "uncertainty." Often, dukkha is translated as "suffering." Whatever the translation, it points to the truth that life is, at times, tremendously difficult and painful. Moreover, circumstances arise and pass away because of causes and conditions, largely out of our control. In 1985, I traveled to Thailand to practice in a forest monastery called Wat Pa Baan Taad. The teacher there, a powerful master of meditation named Ajahn Maha Boowa, defined dukkha as "a constant squeeze." This is the best definition of dukkha I have ever heard. It makes the concept so palpable. This squeeze of life is constant, although we can ignore it for limited periods of time. The problem is that our awareness of it always returns.

The constant squeeze on the heart is because of the inevitability of loss; all beings experience loss. Present loss and the sense of impending loss: both are painful and confining. When we are overtly suffering, we may know this truth clearly. At other times, when things are going well, we may temporarily forget. When the mind becomes quieter, as it does in meditation, this squeeze on the heart becomes apparent. The good news is that we can work with this in our practice.

Although loss always feels utterly personal when we are experiencing it, and in one sense it is, it is also not personal at all. The par-

4

ticularities are different for each of us, but loss is a given for all of us. When we acknowledge this universality, the sense of loneliness and isolation, of alienation and separateness, can ease a bit. Our challenge as contemplative practitioners is to open into the largest perspective possible, without negating, ignoring, or undermining the personal aspects of our own situation in life.

When I first heard this teaching, I experienced deep relief. I realized that I was not alone in my awareness that life is not always so wonderful. The possibility that this was a sign of my connectedness to others was already a cause for ease, even before I began a formal meditation practice.

I was brought up by loving parents who were in sustained emotional pain for much of their lives. My father had to grow up far too quickly, my mother seemed to have a kind of existential anxiety, and I felt everything strongly. I was like a sponge, soaking up everything that happened in my home life, and I tended to experience an immense impact from every event, small and large. I was often buffeted about by huge waves of emotion.

When my father told me I had a sibling who had died before I was born, I was shocked. I found this child's name in the family Bible with the dates of her birth and death. When I learned about the Holocaust and that slavery had existed in our country for over 245 years, I could hardly bear these terrible truths. The emotions of my parents, the facts of this human world, and my own emotional reactions were intense and troubling, but I also sensed the possibility of living differently.

Two repeated experiences led me to this perception. The first such experience was observing my mother in church each Sunday and noticing how she seemed to become an almost totally different person. I watched her shift from focusing on material aspects of life to expressing a seriousness and devotion of being. Especially while taking communion, she was luminous and beautiful in a way that did not show in her everyday life. What I witnessed impressed me deeply and pointed to another dimension of life that I longed to experience.

The second such experience came from encountering silence. One place I learned about the value of silence was at the local library, where my parents often dropped me off. I don't mean to imply that they were neglectful parents. They were not, but they did seem, at times, to forget to pick me back up again. They knew I would be content roaming around on my own and reading whatever I wanted. Spending long stretches of time on my own in the silence of that library, and alone in the chapel of my Catholic elementary school, was the start of a lifelong exploration of silence. Both settings offered a taste of the silence I later found within.

As a child, though I couldn't necessarily express it clearly, I always felt I was losing something such as people, hugs, dolls, bobby pins, food, safety, pleasure, and comfort. I often tried to verbalize this to my family, but it didn't go all that well because my family, like so many, was not very forthcoming. One of the Buddha's own definitions of dukkha suggests that we are often separated from the people we want to be with, and in contact with ones from whom we'd rather be separate. It is not that there were no periods of happiness, even joy, in my childhood, but I spent a lot of time wondering about the oddness of existence, feeling everything in a way that I wasn't able to get away from. Perhaps you have had similar experiences. . . .

Some years ago, I went through a time of great loss in a number of different realms of life. My marriage of twenty-three years dissolved and my father died during the same period. Also, the meditation center for which I am responsible was undergoing great change, and I wasn't sure I could continue to teach there if it changed in ways with which I could not live.

My relationship with my father was resolved long before he died, and so the loss of him, while immense, was also simple. The complexity of being his daughter had eased years before. But the fact that he died at the same time as my marriage ended made his death more painful for me. I had to learn how to depend upon myself after so many years of mutual support with my spouse. It was difficult to disentangle one loss from another. As for the uncertainty at the meditation center, because I was part of its founding and had been guiding it consistently for many years, I felt great grief at the thought of leaving.

For all of us, the conditions in life upon which we depend are bound to shift and dissolve. Sometimes they do this at the same time, and so it was for me. The fact that I had so many years of meditation practice behind me was a blessing. The Dharma was a refuge and a guide in the midst of these conditions. My practice allowed learning to take place, a deeper learning about conditioning and freedom from conditioning. My practice kept me from flailing around or drowning in my sorrow. It's not that I didn't flail at all, as friends would attest. But because of my previous training, I know that the flailing was more conscious and thus less overwhelming than it would have been without the teachings to support and direct me.

When this chain of losses began to happen, I found myself in the midst of great sorrow. But I also found that I was curious, as well as determined. I was curious to discover what the impact of a dedicated practice over the length of forty-some years would have during a difficult time and determined to relate to it all as material for liberation. Two of the great questions are how can we practice in the midst of adversity and what do we unconsciously leave out or dismiss as unworthy of practicing with?

My experiences were, or course, normal human experiences. Heartbreak is heartbreakingly common; the death of one's parents is preordained; and one's work life is often full of great change. My struggles were not due to horrific events and of the most ordinary kind. Yet, it was a truly painful time for me. Because of the nature of my particular conditioning, there was an immensity of sorrow.

At times like this, questions arise: How can we continue in the midst of loss? How can we live and thrive? How can we sustain a basic confidence in life? Moreover, how can we live up to our aspiration to be strong and steady enough within ourselves to bear witness for one another, and do our best to alleviate the immensity of suffering in this world? In short, how can we lead a meaningful life in the very midst of knowing that situations and conditions are always changing and even the best of circumstances will always come to an end?

Because of my previous training in contemplative practice, my reactions to these losses were accompanied by the allies of awareness and illumination, which brought about a greater degree of spaciousness and inner ease than I would have experienced otherwise. I was also aware of the absence of confusion. I knew exactly how to practice with the conditions facing me. And even in the midst of pain, I was struck by a surprising sense of joy. I felt as if my grief were somehow moving through a field of joy, instead of getting stuck and obscuring joy.

Our practice is a response to this world of one loss after another, a way to tune in to a deeper level of reality. When we discover the way things really are, we find true and lasting rest and relief. We learn to practice enjoying conditions (when we can) without clinging to them. In disentangling ourselves from the futile belief that the impermanent can be ultimately satisfying, we turn our attention within.

The teachings of the Buddha and the methods of realizing these teachings are a response to the deepest questions of the heart. Even practicing the methods just a little can improve the quality of our day-to-day life. We get ourselves in less trouble. We cause less trouble for others. We live with more calm. This is no small matter.

If we practice with great intent and dedication, the practice becomes our life. Instead of practice being something we do, it is something we are. We become aware of a great secret treasure within our own hearts: an ease and peace that cannot be destroyed. Of course, this is not really a secret. It has been realized, understood, and taught by countless sages before. However, it is completely different to discover this truth for ourselves than to hear it from others. We meditate to discover that which is beyond conditions. We meditate to tame our minds and to train our hearts to discover, for ourselves, a peace that is truly unconditioned.

The fact that loss is intertwined with life itself doesn't mean we negate or disdain the joys of this world. In fact, because all conditions are impermanent, conditions are to be cherished.

In the same way, the fact that loss is one of the main features of living in this world doesn't negate the value of working for positive change in our spheres of influence. The fact that all of us will eventually lose everything doesn't mean that we should not aspire to create lovely conditions for ourselves and for others. We each have our part to play, and there are infinite ways of working toward positive change. Some will engage in justice work, others will raise children. Some will sit in caves, literally or figuratively, and practice meditation. I believe that if a yogi sitting in a cave meditates with a wise perspective, that yogi is blessing the world through the elimination of greed, hatred, and delusion within their own heart.

One important point to make about loss is that each of us responds differently to the various losses in our lives. A particular circumstance for one person may feel like the worst loss in their lives. For another, that same circumstance may be very painful but not feel quite as utterly devastating. We need to approach our losses and the losses of one another with great compassion and sensitivity, and with a clear sense of nonhierarchy, not judging one loss as greater or lesser than another. It's also important to remember that whether one type of loss is experienced as more important than another is, at least in part, culturally determined. Regardless of culture, however, researchers point out that loss causes physical changes in the body, whatever the object of one's loss might be. In other words, physiological changes are the same, independent of the object of a loss or a culture's decision about how it should be honored.

All loss deserves compassion. Because we are conditioned to compare and to judge, thinking things such as your loss is not as bad as my loss, my loss is not as valid as your loss, your or my loss isn't really even a loss at all, it is possible to lose sight of the fact that all loss is painful. As human beings, we are all subject to conditioning, though we are subject to different kinds of conditioning because our individual makeups and environments vary. Because our experiences tap into our conditioning, what one may imagine on the outside is someone else's "overreaction" to their loss is always going to be, from the inside, simply an appropriate response.

The object of loss is never unimportant to the one who experiences the loss. And a meditative approach includes looking at our relationship to loss. Understanding our relationship to a loss can free the heart. It can lead to a greater understanding and a wider perspective, the kind of understanding that brings real peace to our hearts. This understanding is exactly what the teachings of the Buddha point to: the teachings have only and everything to do with our lives as they are. And for all of us, our lives as they are will include loss.

Times of great loss are like thickets in which we can lose ourselves—and they are also full of the potential of awakening to the recognition that loss is inherent in life. On the other side of "things as they are" is a path of joy, so don't imagine the Buddha's path is one of resignation. In his time, the Buddha was asked why he and his disciples were so radiant, because clearly, their practice had brought them great ease and deep joy.

The Buddha's path is one of immeasurable joy. Recalling this and having confidence in this are essential because meditating is sometimes quite difficult. We find our way into suffering only to discover a pathway that leads into previously unimaginable spaciousness. Many words have been written about this truth, but words can never accurately describe it because it is about our lives, our hearts, and the very heart of things. As we meditate, we explore painful subjects, and we do so because these painful subjects have an immense impact on our lives. Without attending carefully, we will always feel caught by the conditions of this world. Attending carefully, we can discover what is referred to in the Bible as "the peace that passeth all understanding."

We experience daily life losses seemingly around every corner, during which low-level grief reactions occur. Attending to such losses, we can be aware that loss is intertwined with life. We gain, and then we lose what has been gained. We succeed, and then we fail. And maybe we feel that up until now, we have lived an impoverished life. We have not gained or succeeded at much of anything.

Sometimes, however, losses are deeply traumatic. Such loss is a different matter. When we experience great loss, all of the other losses of our lives tend to re-arise. Although the mind grips onto the object of the current loss, the undigested emotional material of our past losses arises in consciousness as well. We lose what we feel we just cannot afford to lose, and yet we lose it all the same. We lose what we feel we cannot live without. We think we may not survive if we lose *this*, whatever the *this* is.

Many people, even when conditions are okay or even great, live waiting for the other shoe to drop, whatever that other shoe might be. Even if we have a sense that we will survive because we have to survive, we may be afraid that the depth of the loss will leave us so impoverished, so deprived, we will be unable to thrive. Loss is one of the hardest aspects of being human, of being embodied. The other shoe will always drop.

Dharma practice holds open another way of meeting loss, even great loss, which is to accept it as part of our path. In recognizing loss as not only a problem but also as a path, something new opens up. In the willingness to sustain our attention and remain openhearted in the midst of the pain, in our willingness to turn toward instead of away from, in the intention to open and embrace and allow our hearts to break, a path of liberation becomes visible. This is a path of joy.

....

Be ahead of all parting, as though it already were
behind you, like the winter that has just gone by.
For among these winters there is one so endlessly winter
that only by wintering through it will your heart survive.
—*Rainer Maria Rilke*

....

In the midst of pain, it is difficult to trust and be confident that turning toward the difficult is actually the way out. Given our past experiences, we come by our avoidance honestly. Yet, turning toward is what is called for, taking what can feel like a risk and summoning up attentiveness in the midst of the difficult. We don't need to be dramatic about it. We need just enough attentiveness to steady ourselves and sustain awareness, while life does what it does. The practice is to steady ourselves in the here and now, in the environment in which we find ourselves, while grief is flowing in and out.

Practice means pausing to ask, *What does life want of me right now?* instead of *What do I want to get out of life?* When we ask the latter question, we are setting ourselves up for more suffering, because conditions do not tend to cooperate with our personal agendas. And yet, we don't quite believe this obvious fact, and so we try to control life and do everything possible to make life cooperate, trying to *get something out of* conditions instead of surrendering to what is being asked of us here and now.

What is being asked of us is always the same thing: Is it possible to be aware? Is it possible to not shut down and dwell in our thoughts, but to be present with what is?

We are asked to have enough confidence and trust to continue to expose what is happening—the intensity of grief, for example—to the light of awareness. We are asked to understand that it is not all *on us* to do the work: awareness does its own work. Wisdom does its own work, as we do our best to simply remain attentive.

We see change most vividly, perhaps, within the forms of life that we have chosen over time. I have taught in one Dharma center for over thirty years so I have a long perspective. I have seen a lot of change. The center I am responsible for has changed on every level. Staff have come and gone; teachers have come and gone; and most vividly, vast numbers of practitioners have come and gone. A number of practitioners have died; people have moved away; people have fallen in love and think they no longer need to practice (though these, at least, usually come back). People have fallen out of love and feel that only one partner has "dibs" on the center. People change traditions, and people stop practicing altogether. A large number of people have come through the doors just once, never to be seen again. And, at the same time, there is a steady and dedicated population of practitioners who depend on the center and on one another to continue to develop their hearts.

All of this portrays Ajahn Maha Boowa's "constant squeeze." This constant squeeze is inherent in the human condition. It is the first of the ennobling truths that the Buddha discovered and taught.

But this squeeze can be released. In fact the very reason we are here on this earth is to release this squeeze. Releasing this squeeze is the fruition of this path of liberation. One way that Ajahn Maha Boowa described liberation was as "enoughness." This path moves from the recognition of a constant squeeze toward knowing enoughness within our own hearts.

The rest of the book will investigate this movement into enoughness.

2

The Five Recollections

THE BUDDHA SPOKE ABOUT THE inevitability of loss in a variety of ways throughout his teaching life. He also described a way to practice with the fact of loss. The practice is called the five recollections and is described in the Upajjhatthana Sutta.

> I am of the nature to age.
> Aging is unavoidable.
>
> I am of the nature to get ill.
> Illness is unavoidable.
>
> I am of the nature to die.
> Death is unavoidable.
>
> All that is dear to me and everyone I love
> are of the nature to change.
> There is no way to escape being separated from them.

My actions are my only true belongings.
I cannot avoid the consequences of my actions.
My actions are the ground on which I stand.

The Buddha encouraged everyone, lay and ordained, woman or man, to contemplate these five realities on a daily basis. His awareness of these facts was a catalyst for him, in his yearning for ultimate freedom. In the story of the Buddha's life it is said that what motivated him to leave the familiarity and comfort of his daily life, which held for him a future of wealth and power, was coming face to face with someone old, someone sick, and someone dead. The contact with loss in the forms of old age, sickness, and death motivated him to change his life into one that held little of the security to which he had been accustomed. And yet, he knew he needed to make a leap if he were ever to find the peace he was seeking. Our path is the same. Contemplating these realities of life motivates us to make necessary changes. Allowing these contemplations to sink into the heart is itself a deeply beneficial practice.

Our inquiry begins with the first four of the five recollections. They are facts of life, even if we are inclined to do our best to ignore them. The practice of deliberately bringing them to mind and reflecting on their reality may seem counterintuitive. Why would anyone want to reflect on these seemingly dark realities? Would not doing so make us gloomy or even depressed? So it may seem, but the fact is that we can save ourselves a great deal of suffering if we choose to live in accordance with them.

Contemplating these recollections encourages us to awaken from denial and avoidance. The recollections offer a pathway of nonattachment and equanimity and a deeper, more sustained appreciation of this moment, now. A lightness of being emerges when we face what is undeniably so. If we take these recollections up as a practice, we are deliberately calling these realities forth instead of simply being at their mercy, overwhelmed by the thoughts and emotions they activate.

To recollect these facts brings about a sense of spiritual urgency, known in Pali as *samvega*. Samvega inspires us to practice with zeal, with passion and dedication, but without striving or ambition. Spiritual urgency, the urgency to free the heart, needs to be accompanied by another quality, *pasada*, which is a confidence in that which is not conditioned. Together, these open us to the reality that inner freedom is a very real possibility in this life.

We take up the truths of the five remembrances as a practice, as a way to deepen our insight. Through practice we can come to see that each one manifests in both personal and universal ways. Each one is either true for me right now or will be true for me in the future, and at the same time they are all true for all of us. When practicing the contemplations, it is sometimes beneficial to use the pronoun *I* and at other times, *we*. Using *we* helps us expand our perspective and realize we are not alone. This realization reminds us that it is not a fault to get sick and to age. We are not separate from nature.

Ajahn Maha Boowa expressed this understanding poignantly when he was in a potentially life-threatening situation. During his life as a monk in the forests of Thailand, tigers were abundant. Monks often heard the roar of tigers in the distance as they sat meditating under their mosquito nets. Ajahn Maha Boowa once came upon a tiger while walking in meditation in the forest. He met this tiger with these words: "Greetings, comrade in old age, sickness, and death!"

Perhaps the tiger felt their kinship as beings. In any case, the tiger went on its way.

All sentient beings, without exemption, are subject to these natural laws. This body is not ultimately in our control. This body belongs to nature. Even this mind isn't in our control. We cannot choose what arises. This mind belongs to nature. What happens when a deeper understanding of how little control we really do have leads to a diminishing or dropping out of the sense of self? Old age, sickness, and death are not dukkha if they are not clung to as *I* or *me* or *mine*. When we see clearly that illness and death are not *I, me,* or *mine*, the dukkha that they ordinarily cause may lessen a great deal or even cease altogether.

....

THE FIRST RECOLLECTION IS: "I am of the nature to age. Aging is unavoidable."

Older people sometimes say: "In my time, this or that happened" or "In my time, I was like this or that." How is this moment not our time if we are alive? The phrase *in my time* points, they perhaps imagine, to a time when life was full with family and friends, with work or career. When people say this, they often mean that contemporary culture has become too difficult to understand or that because the body/mind is degenerating, my "real" time was at some point in the past when I was young and healthy. The older person saying this may feel invisible now. In a culture that fears death, we feel invisible as we age in a way that wasn't so when we were younger. One of the many saving graces of the Buddha's teaching is that if you are alive, every moment is your time.

By the time my father died at the age of ninety-one, he had gone to many funerals. Ten years before he died, my mother died. Just after she died, my father confided in me that he felt old for the first time, even though he was already eighty-two. He said he felt he was "beyond his time." In fact, he went on to have two more intimate relationships and countless contacts with family and friends. He traveled to New Zealand and was passionately interested in the world. He used to call me up to discuss President Obama's economic policies. And, this is how he felt just after losing my mother. I wondered then whether his fear of disconnection was part of his process of grieving my mother, manifesting in this feeling of being old.

There are conventional positive aspects to aging as well. After all, not much is just one thing, good or bad, though it can look one way or the other. A chaplain in a hospital in New York, when visiting a woman who was ninety-six, asked her how life was at her age. "Terrific," she said. "There's no peer pressure."

....

One purpose of our practice is to enjoy our old age. But
we can't fool ourselves. Only sincere practice will work.

—*Shunryu Suzuki*

....

As for practice, the forms practice takes sometimes need to shift as we age. Whatever posture of meditation we need to support our practice as we age is the best posture. And, as we get older, the essence of practice can burn even brighter as we come face to face with loss. This is the time to adjust the forms of practice in ways that work for us. It is imperative to practice with an open mind, free from expectations, and to embrace without compromise the aspiration to awaken.

As we learn to accept the natural limitations of this body/mind experience, it becomes ever more possible to live with greater love and wonder and with less clinging and attachment. This is the sign of a true contemplative, not just a person who can sit endlessly on a cushion.

It is easy to get lost in concepts of time and age, believing in conventional messages. However, many older practitioners have practiced for much of their lives. Their dedication to the practice makes it possible to meet physical and mental limitations from a radically different perspective than the ordinary one. Many people say that their greatest age-related fear is losing their minds. Nisargadatta Maharaj, a great sage who lived India in the twentieth century, was once asked what it was like for him when people noticed him becoming forgetful. He said he knew he wasn't his mind, so losing his mind wasn't a problem. He understood that he was only losing what was never his to begin with.

This could indeed be seen as cold comfort for those of us not as evolved! However, a quite ordinary practitioner whom I've worked with for many years came to me some years ago with a diagnosis of mental deterioration. I offered him the teaching that he is not his mind, which he initially resisted. He then decided to trust me, and take the words in deeply. As he tried applying this teaching, he felt a peace that has never left him, though his mind continues to deteriorate. Perhaps this teaching is applicable not just to those we consider to be special.

In times of change, there is often a sense of loss as well. In opening and allowing the grief that accompanies loss, a deeper dignity can emerge. What are your ideas and concepts about what practice is and what it means? Is practice something separate from the rest of your life? Is it possible to open your heart to things as they are, whatever way they are?

Older practitioners with a lifelong practice have a hard-won wisdom. They are the visible signs of the humanness of life as well as the possibility of transcendence. We practice for others as well as ourselves. Older practitioners need more commitment and diligence than ever before as they continue to age.

The second recollection is: "I am of the nature to get sick. Sickness is unavoidable."

Even the very young may know they can get sick or disabled at any time. As we age, even if we are generally quite healthy, there is no guarantee we will remain that way. I have heard many times that people are not as much afraid of death as they are of disability. If you are disabled now, using this reflection on illness may help to alleviate the isolation and feelings of alienation that so easily occur. Conditions in our lives can change instantly. We are comrades in old age, sickness, and death.

Along with old age and death, sickness (and disability) is known as a heavenly messenger because it is part of the story of the Buddha's first entry into the world of sorrow and pain. When the Buddha encountered these visually, in the sight of an aged person, an ill person, and a dead body, he received the message that he and all whom he loved would also get sick, age, and die. This truth became very clear.

He realized that he needed to live in a different way, a way that would support inquiring into that which is not subject to death, his own inherently peaceful deathless nature. As we know, illness and disability are possibilities for all of us, no matter how healthy we are in this moment. The poet Susan Sontag puts it this way: "Everyone who is born holds dual citizenship, in the kingdom of the well and in the kingdom of the sick."

Seeing people who are sick or disabled reminds us of our own vulnerability. Because we don't want to be reminded, the reality of "shooting the messenger" is familiar to those who are disabled. I hear story after story about abuse being heaped on people with disabilities. The abuse appears to be one of the most painful aspects of disability, beyond the disability itself. If those of us not yet disabled can let go of the self-centered fear of becoming disabled, we are more apt to treat those who are with the greatest of respect, doing whatever we can to affirm the dignity and sacred spark in all beings.

The third of the recollections is: "I am of the nature to die. Death is unavoidable."

What is our relationship to death? Do we try to push it away and forget about it or does the idea of dying haunt us?

In the Sattipathana Sutta, a major discourse, the Buddha instructs us to pay attention to the body as a foundational way of being present. Practicing mindfulness of the body is a lifelong practice. And the reality is that the body itself will drop away at some point.

My friend Sarah is ninety, and she has been a dedicated practitioner since the age of fifty-five, when she discovered this path. She began participating in lengthy silent retreats, and in the space of ten years, she sat ten retreats of three months each. Now, at the age of ninety, she lives in assisted living housing. Whenever I visit her, I learn vital lessons about practicing into old age.

Recently, on a visit, she told me she is practicing charnel grounds contemplation—reflections on death—as described in the Satipatthana Sutta. She said that before moving from her home into this assisted living, she had thought she was already aware of how quickly death can come. However, in assisted living, the reality that the body and mind are impermanent was hitting home in a deeper way. During the years she has lived in this environment, more than twelve good friends have died. She tells me that each death deepens her understanding that the nature of the body is to pass away.

Each time a good friend dies she grieves. Many people in her situation would decide not to get close to other residents, given the fact that they will likely soon be gone. She has decided to keep her heart open to new friendships nonetheless. She realizes that the cost of closing her heart would be far more painful than the emotional pain of loss, so she keeps choosing connection.

I was able to be with both of my parents as they died, and I accompanied their bodies to the crematorium. I felt called to do this, given their care of my body before I was able to care for it myself. With each parent, I recited prayers for their ongoing journey, while pushing the button that began the process of bodily disintegration, and then meditated in the cemetery until the cremations were complete. My intent was to honor them, not to practice cemetery contemplation. Yet, inevitably, sitting in contemplation as their bodies dissolved was a deep and profound contemplation on death.

The fourth recollection is an interesting one: "All that is dear to me and everyone I love are of the nature to change. There is no way to escape being separated from them."

It seems to me that the Buddha decided that in case we didn't get this teaching on aging, illness, and death after hearing the first three contemplations, he would drive the message home with the fourth. This fourth recollection can hit harder than the previous three. We know the truth of the first three, even if we turn away from them. The fourth recollection reminds us that we won't only lose our youth, beauty, health, and bodies, and minds. We will lose *everyone* and *everything* in our lives that we cherish.

This fourth and most provocative reflection asks us to be aware that we will lose whatever we may have gained. It means losing relationships to death, separation, and geography but also, of course, losing our health, money, career, and material belongings—everything we think we can own.

It might be helpful to pause at this point and consider that while the fourth recollection sounds as dark as can be, the path is a way to greater ease and inner freedom. None of this sounds all that cheerful, and yet, because it is true, it can be met as a relief. Because it is true, we can start to do what we can to find a way out, just as the Buddha did. The way out is the path of love, free from grasping.

These first four recollections can be viewed as wake-up calls. We are initiated into life as it is when we lose what we love and are dependent upon, while at the same time sustaining our awareness as it happens. When we lose what we love, it's not simply an experience of loss. It is also a marker, an opening to understanding what we have ignored or denied with a kind of willful ignorance.

The first four contemplations address loss and instability. The fifth is the opposite. It has to do with stability and possibility, what we can do to move in the direction of inner freedom. It asks for deep and thoughtful contemplation.

The fifth recollection is this: "My actions are my only true belongings. I cannot avoid the consequences of my actions. My actions are the ground on which I stand."

This contemplation expresses the understanding of causes and consequences, the understanding that skillful actions bring inner ease and unskillful actions bring suffering. This reminder of the importance of caring for actions of body, speech, and mind is deeply beneficial. What we do and do not do matters. This is not to say that life is not sometimes quite complicated; it is not always so simple to know what to do. But if we keep this recollection in mind, we can embrace the complexity, making the best choices we can.

This moment is the ground on which we stand. Whatever actions we have or have not engaged in, the present moment is the moment that matters. This is the moment that conditions the next moment, and the moment after that. To be present and awake right now is the message of the fifth recollection. While we cannot change the past, we can make wise choices here and now.

Another way to understand this reflection is to see that it is always possible, under any condition, to care for the heart. Under the weight of difficult conditions, caring for our hearts is sometimes all we can do. To care for the heart is to care for what is most important to learn and understand and release in this life. We use the exact conditions in our own lives as the path forward. What inspires us most are not words about the Dharma, but our lived experience of its truth. In this way, we are paying attention to the heart of the matter.

Caring for the heart means learning and applying the teachings of the Buddha, which are simply the teachings of reality, of life, to clear away that which obscures and veils the heart. The Buddha said that the heart is already awake within each one of us. We need to know this truth thoroughly for ourselves.

There are a number of ways to practice with these five recollections. One is to put the list of them somewhere prominent—on your refrigerator, for instance, as I have done—so that you have no choice but to look at them. I believe this is known in the suttas as "refrigerator practice." Or it would be, if there had been refrigerators in the Buddha's time. Other ways are to begin each sitting session by inwardly recollecting each one, pausing to open to its implications, and moving to the next. They can be practiced in this way while sitting or walking, as well as while lying in bed ready for sleep. Another way to practice is to contemplate each fact briefly before getting out of bed each morning. Reciting each recollection aloud can also be beneficial.

The point of this practice is not to make it hard to get out of bed. If working with these recollections causes hopelessness or resignation, the time is not right to work with them. Better to wait until there is more inner balance.

We recall these facts of nature in order to live our lives with a greater sense of aliveness, to recognize that this moment, and every moment, matters. To reflect on these five recollections is to make loss into a path of inner liberation. We do so by letting go of attachment in regard to the first four contemplations and by recognizing how essential it is to practice the fifth recollection of wisdom and compassion, right here and right now.

3

Magnanimous Heart

....

Magnanimous Heart is like a mountain, stable and impartial. Exemplifying the ocean, it is tolerant and views everything from the broadest perspective. Having a magnanimous heart means being without prejudice and refusing to take sides. When carrying something that weighs an ounce, do not think of it as light, and likewise, when you have to carry fifty pounds, do not think of it as heavy. Do not get carried away by the sounds of spring, nor become heavy-hearted upon seeing the colors of fall. View the changes of the seasons as a whole, and weigh the relativeness of light and heavy from a broad perspective.

—Dogen
....

ABOUT A YEAR AFTER MY time of so many losses, I went to talk to a teacher whom I trusted and respected. I asked him: How can I possibly endure these losses? How can I relate to this time of multiple losses as the Dharma? Is it possible to understand loss differently than I do now? What can I do about this grief?

The teacher heard me out and then said, "There is no such thing as loss."

I said, "Really?"

His translator was translating his words from Chinese into English, so I thought either he hadn't understood me or I hadn't understood him. Also, I had hoped for a different answer because I had no idea what "no such thing as loss" could possibly mean.

So I asked the same question again. His answer was the same.

The grief I was experiencing made his words impossible to accept. But I knew him as a kind and compassionate person, whose life was dedicated to alleviating suffering, so I wanted to try to investigate what he meant.

Thankfully, I had been practicing for decades. If I had been new to the practice, I would have thought he was either crazy or cruel, or that the Dharma had no relevance to actual human life. But because of my respect for him and because I also knew he had experienced great loss himself, I was intrigued and began to contemplate his statement. As I investigated, I opened to another perspective that was more expansive than any I had encountered before.

How can there possibly be no such thing as loss? Obviously there is loss! Our reactions to loss signal the reality of loss. To say that loss does not exist does not ring true, especially when a loss has a direct impact on our lives or the lives of those whom we love.

In the initial shock of a great loss, our mission is simply to live through it as best we can. Our meditative task is to bring the utmost compassion to each and every loss, our own losses or the losses of others. The only reasonable response is compassion.

What I realized, after working with what he had said, is that this teacher was speaking from an entirely different framework and had a very different perspective. If we look through this other lens, we can see that when we use the word *loss*, we turn a living experience into a concept.

From our usual point of view, we understand that the absence of what we once had is a loss, while from another vantage point it is simply life unfolding according to nature, in its own way and according to its own laws, regardless of how we would prefer things to be. From this second viewpoint, loss is simply the irrefutable fact of change.

Unlike this teacher, I myself would not say there is no such thing as loss, although I also understand that his perspective offers us an opportunity to expand our view of loss. We can open our minds to this more expansive way of understanding it. And, at times, this perspective reveals itself to us without any personal effort on our parts. We understand it intuitively.

Seeing loss in this way is an expression of "magnanimous heart," as the thirteenth-century Zen master Dogen puts it. The Buddha's teachings point to the biggest perspective possible: a heart of magnanimity. Magnanimous heart is a heart of balance and buoyancy. It allows us to approach each moment exactly as it is, in a fresh and alive way and free from agendas about how it should be. Magnanimous heart is a generous heart, a benevolent heart, a heart of inclusivity in which there is room for all that arises and we receive all that we encounter.

Magnanimous heart has the capacity to hold anything and everything with openheartedness. It embraces all conditions with equanimity, helping us to be with what is instead of getting lost in our opinions of *good* and *bad*. We can also call this *awareness*.

Magnanimous heart operates like a swinging door. Experiences come in and experiences go out, without clinging or interpretation. We digest and release experiences, instead of getting caught in ideas about the way things are and how they "should" be or finding fault with ourselves or others.

This way of being allows us to encounter what is present with spaciousness. Buoyancy allows us to be not stuck to the content of each moment, to each sense perception. Whatever is here is here; held in magnanimous heart it flows through us with kindness and compassion, gentleness and tenderness. When we take this spacious approach, vulnerability becomes an asset instead of a problem because all is allowed and released. Vulnerability allows us to receive experiences without resistance. Relaxing into spaciousness, we allow each experience, whether pleasant or painful, to be received and released. We are open to the next moment's experience.

The practice of insight meditation is a process of opening—to this moment, to our heartfelt aspirations, to one another. To completely open our heart and mind in this way is, in a certain sense, to be like the Buddha. As the practice opens us to what has been closed away and unconscious, we become willing to learn how to shift our views and try to understand loss from different points of view.

Etty Hillesum, who died in Auschwitz at the age of twenty-nine, wrote this: "If you don't understand while you're here that all outer experiences are like a passing show, as nothing beside the great splendor inside us—then things can look very bleak here indeed." This great splendor is magnanimous heart.

Practice encourages us to see how it is possible to turn the sting and anguish of loss into a path of liberation. Most of the time, we try our best to avoid loss and to magnify or prolong what we view as gain. Practice encourages us to investigate whether there is another way to respond than our fallback, the conditioned view to which we've been bound. Instead of allowing a loss to solidify our conditioning, can it be a springboard for seeing experiences in different ways, in ways that bring about inner freedom?

One of the most fruitful arenas of investigation is the inquiry into the ways we relate to loss. This kind of inquiry enables us to see for ourselves that loss itself and the various ways of relating to it are separate. There is loss, and there is our relationship to loss, which is separate from the experience of loss itself. Inquiring into one's relationship to loss is the exit sign, pointing to a way in which our relationship to loss can shift. In shifting, our experience of life is transformed.

A vital question to inquire into is whether we believe that loss intrinsically diminishes us and makes us less than we were before a loss. Our conditioning naturally leads us to feel diminished by a loss. After all, how would loss not diminish us? When we have lost what we think and feel is essential to our well-being and happiness, how can loss not diminish our lives and identity?

But when we lose what we feel we need to have—and it is a *when* and not an *if*—are we truly diminished? Is loss all that there is; is life only loss? Or can we relate differently to loss and grief? If we define ourselves by the conditions we are in, we will surely be diminished when those conditions change or fall away. If we consider the conditions in our lives and this body/mind experience to be who we are—*I, me, mine* in a solid and significant way, as if we have control over them—then yes, we are diminished in the face of loss.

But do we have to be defined by conditions? Is defining ourselves by the conditions in our lives inevitable in the same way that loss itself is inevitable? We can enjoy the things of life. We can appreciate conditions in our lives. Just the fact of being alive is precious and wondrous. And we can recognize that in defining ourselves by conditions, we will always live in turbulence, discontent, and the sense that something is always wrong.

To meditate is to train ourselves to turn our attention within, to find a peace that is independent of conditions. One point of our practice is to develop confidence in the fact that we must look within. Of course, this is a basic Dharma point, actually the most basic of Dharma points, but we have to know it deeply in our bones. And then we have to *live* it, however challenging it may be at times.

....

The Dharma is directly visible, timeless,
calling one to come see for oneself.

—*The Buddha*

....

The path of liberation is an invitation to find out whether we are condemned to a life in which experiences of loss define existence. No one is exempt from loss, and yet, being diminished by loss is not inevitable. We can move and shift and change and transform and transcend our experiences of loss through understanding and opening, through embodying the practice. We allow the picture as we initially see it to get bigger. In so doing, we see that we have never really owned anything at all and thus cannot lose what we never really had.

Our practice is to recognize and engage with the reality of our lives, to find a way through loss to peace and inner wholeness. We make of our lives a path to understanding. All experiences in our lives are the very practice itself, and it is essential to place our attention on the very experiences that we would rather leave out.

Encountering loss from the perspective of the Dharma and from the perspective of the practice clarifies the path. Clarifying the path means that the path becomes more visible. If we are oriented in a direction of inner freedom, each encounter, every experience, brings us more and more inner freedom. As we learn to release and allow, we also learn to trust and encourage the process of relinquishment.

This approach takes us beyond survival, though simply surviving in the immediacy of overwhelming loss may be all that is possible in some moments. On the most basic level, our task is to endure until life has a chance to teach us what we need to know, and what we need to know is the kind of safety and trust that lies within and is beyond conditions. We need to let life teach us and guide us lovingly into this terrain of loss and transformation.

What we need to know within our bones is that we cannot really cling to anything because clinging won't make it stay. In the experience of a loss, what we have mistakenly depended upon becomes extremely clear. It becomes so highlighted in consciousness that we sideline and cast aside other aspects of life that we also value. Sometimes, until we lose what we've mistakenly depended upon, we don't know the extent of our dependence. After all, what could be more human than depending on that which is dear and beloved? At the same time, nothing external, nothing conditioned, can ultimately sustain us.

When we clearly see this, loss can bring greater inner wholeness, the sense that we are complete within ourselves. With attentiveness and calm, in working with loss carefully and compassionately, we discover a sense of completion within ourselves. The dissolving of what we depended upon leaves a space, and this space is where we discover our inner wholeness. Wholeness is found within this empty space. The falling away of a condition we were dependent upon makes this space visible. We may not have been aware of this space because we were unconsciously leaning on a particular condition to hold us up. When conditions let us down, we may discover this space within.

When what we've been leaning against falls away, there is a void. In the void of not having the condition to depend upon anymore, we can see what has been unseen. Ungraspable spaciousness and love have always been present, but dependence on conditions clouds perception.

I recognize that from a conventional point of view this way of looking at loss may seem absurd. Conventionally speaking, with each loss in life, we feel we are diminished more and more. Especially as we get older, it seems obvious that we are ever more diminished. But from another point of view, there actually is no diminishment or, as the teacher I referred to earlier put it, "no such thing as loss." If we see under appearances, under how things seem to be, we can allow ourselves to rest with great steadiness, silence, and affection in the space that has opened.

We can relax and soften into what grips the heart, letting it release itself through the kindness of attention. This attention is not cold attention, but kind attention, caring attention, loving attention; this attention lets sorrow release itself in its own way and in its own time. We become aware of the resistance that causes the grip to get stronger and can gradually relax even that resistance.

In the experience of loss, we find that many of the beliefs we had previously held don't sustain and support us as they did before we were under such stress. For example, we may have believed, quite unconsciously, that it is possible to know the future and that we know our future to be bright. Now we fall into beliefs about a future that is dire. We convince ourselves that this is how life will be, although we can never know what will happen beyond this moment. The liberating alternative is to allow beliefs regarding both a bright future and a dire future to collapse.

We deeply relax, returning to the actuality of being here—the actuality of just sitting; of just breathing; of just sensing, seeing, feeling, thinking, tasting. We return to the simple experience of life as it is, right here and now, not how it was and not how it may be. Thoughts of past and future pull our attention away from attending to what is right here. When we notice such thoughts, we can return to the actuality of what is.

In the encounters with the most painful of thoughts, the most painful of emotions, I suggest inquiring into what other mind states are occurring as well. For example, in the presence of sadness and of fear, I encourage you to look for kindness and love. I don't mean trying to make ourselves *feel* loving but recognizing that, in the midst of the pain, love is also present. This is because love is always present. If we focus on fear and become overwhelmed by it, all we see is more fear; fear has center stage. If we deliberately look for love, love is discovered. To practice in this way is not denying or repressing painful emotions, and it is not pretending our experience is other than what it is. But when we broaden our field of awareness, we see elements of experience that lie alongside the pain, such as love.

In the midst of fear, kindness is needed, even just a little, so that the panic, restlessness, and angst don't completely take over. We can simply ask ourselves if even in the midst of contraction and tension spaciousness is available as well. In the midst of anger, is compassion present? Is there peacefulness in the midst of agitation?

We are not *concocting* anything with these investigations. We are just seeing more clearly what is in fact already there. Because love is our true nature, we will experience love if we open to the presence of love. Maybe it's just a drop of love, not necessarily angels trumpeting, but a drop. That drop is enough to shift perspective. When a painful mental state is strong, please ask yourself: *What else is happening right here and now?*

The Chan master Sheng Yen once pointed out: "Nothing within you has anything to do with you." How radical! We tend to think *everything* has everything to do with us: each thought, reaction, emotion, sensation, and external events as well. We take everything personally. From a conventional psychological point of view, it is of course true that what happens within us is personal. In this regard, psychological work is important, and we need to take responsibility for what we see when we do that work. On the conventional level, there is content to everything and that content needs to be respected.

Our losses aren't just vague and amorphous. And, at the same time, the content is not the total picture.

From a meditative point of view, what we see within is *just a thought, just a reaction, just an emotion, just a sensation.* Sense impressions arise because of conditions coming together, some of which we may know (or think we know), although many cannot be known. What arises is both consequential and inconsequential. This is the view from the perspective of magnanimous heart. It reveals the bigger picture. We might call it a bigger container that can hold the changing conditions in life. Magnanimous heart is contact with an infinite spaciousness of mind.

The Thai forest master Ajahn Chah said: "If you see states rising and falling in the mind and do not cling to the process, letting go of both happiness and suffering, mental rebirths become shorter and shorter. Letting go, you can even fall into hell states without too much disturbance because you know the impermanence of them. Through wise practice you allow your old karma to wear itself out. Knowing how things arise and pass away, you can be aware and let them run their course. It is like having two trees. If you fertilize and water one and do not take care of the other, there is no question which one will grow and which one will die."

If there is one thing we can count on in this uncertain existence, it is that everything conditional is transitory. Everything is temporary and is always in the process of changing. When change is wanted, we are delighted, excited, and happy. It is so lovely.

When change is unwanted and painful, we call it loss, and we are sad, distressed, and dismayed. From a magnanimous-heart point of view, how we want things to be is simply an *opinion*. Conditions are conditions, doing what conditions do, which is change. It is not our fault or anyone's fault. It is not some fault in the universe. The very nature of conditions is to change, and to change, quite often, in unwanted ways.

....

Even now,
decades after,
I wash my face with cold water—

Not for discipline,
nor memory,
nor the icy awakening slap,

but to practice
choosing
to make the unwanted wanted.

      —*Jane Hirshfield*
....

The Buddha's invitation is to discover that which doesn't change. Remaining conscious, staying awake in the midst of both the beautiful and the painful, offers an entry point into the changeless. The changeless is what the Buddha also referred to as the deathless, the unborn, the unconditioned, or the timeless.

Again turning to Master Sheng Yen: "No matter how great a loss is, if you fully accept it straight on, that loss will turn out to be a gain."

In our growing capacity to embrace loss, we come to recognize that loss strengthens our inner resources. Compassion comes forth to meet loss, and because of coming forth, compassion is strengthened. Courage and love are called forth to meet what is happening. Beautiful qualities of heart meet the hole in the heart, the heart that is aching. In this way, love is strengthened, patience is strengthened, and courage is strengthened. We might call this a gain.

Etty Hillesum wrote the following in reference to her fellow prisoners in Auschwitz: "Most people here are much worse off than they need be because they write off their longing for friends and family as so many losses in their lives, when they should count the fact that their heart is able to long so hard and to love so much among their greatest blessings."

In the buoyancy of magnanimous heart, we recognize that everything that occurs is an expression of life. This perspective allows us to stop assessing, measuring, and comparing. We neither add nor subtract from the present moment experience. If we are not fixated on or stuck in concepts of *better* and *worse*, we find that our capacity to respond with greater wisdom and compassion kicks in naturally. We find creative ways and options to meet the way things are. We allow creativity to flow forth. In the simplicity of present moment attentiveness, thoughts arise but we don't feed those thoughts by adding a thought to the thought that is arising.

In returning again and again to the simplicity of being, seeing, breathing, sensing, feeling, and just experiencing, we experience a fundamental interconnectedness. We know this interconnectedness because of allowing the bare experience of life itself to take precedence over concepts and descriptions of life. This shift is the movement from "my life" to life itself. Life itself is just what it is. It is not a problem. Life may be extremely painful at times, but this is the nature of life, to be both pleasant and painful. It is when we think of life as *mine* that life is problematic.

Of course there is loss; there is great loss, in this life.

Yet magnanimous heart holds *all* experiences, including loss, with immeasurable spaciousness. In the recognition of magnanimous mind, we recognize our fundamental goodness. Our engagement and participation in the world begin to shift from viewing this world as a field of consumption to experiencing this world as a field of appreciation.

And we can't help but bow down in gratitude.

PART II

Grief

4

Practicing with Painful Emotions

SO FAR, I'VE ADDRESSED DIFFERENT ways of looking at and
working with loss. The next four chapters delve into ways of responding wisely to the painful emotions that arise in the face of loss.

In the midst of loss, we experience many different painful emotions, not just grief. We experience panic, fear, anger, loneliness,
depression, jealousy, despair, rage, anxiety, shame, boredom, and
other very painful states. In the teachings, painful emotions are
sometimes referred to as the *afflictive emotions* or the *torments of
heart*. Learning to see these energies clearly, and liberating the heart
from their grip, is a true gift of the Dharma. To know we can work
with our own hearts and minds is to find the circumstances in our
lives to be workable.

When I first began to meditate and study the Buddha's teaching
many years ago, I was having problems communicating with a good
friend. She and I had been close, but we had begun to see important
things differently and our friendship was under great stress. At the

same time, I was becoming friends with Larry Rosenberg, a Buddhist teacher who lived nearby.

Before meeting Larry, I had been part of a yoga tradition in which we didn't talk about suffering. Instead we talked about love and light. Entering a different tradition in which the word *suffering* was tossed around casually was, to my ears, shocking, and it took me quite a while before I could begin to understand what those using it meant. Many people around me appeared to be having an okay time, and this word didn't always seem to fit with reality.

At some point I had a conversation with Larry about this interpersonal conflict with my friend. He said to me with great sympathy: "I am so sorry that you are suffering."

I replied, "What? Suffering? I'm not suffering. I just hate her!"

I didn't understand then that anger was actually a form of suffering and that we sometimes inadvertently harm others and ourselves because we do not know how to care for our emotions and work with our minds. The journey from nonawareness to awareness of suffering is the path of the Dharma.

All great sages, including the Buddha, speak about an inherent peacefulness within all of us. As Padmasambhava, an eighth-century Indian Buddhist master, said: "Your original nature has been shining within you all this time. Look within and find out whether or not this is true."

Or as Ajahn Chah says: "In truth there is nothing wrong with this mind. It is intrinsically pure. Within itself it is already peaceful. If the mind is not peaceful, it's because it follows moods. The real mind doesn't have anything to it; it is simply an aspect of nature. It becomes peaceful or agitated because moods deceive it."

We can begin our exploration of this path of liberation with the confidence that all beings are originally peaceful, rather than originally sinful, despite what many of us have been taught. Our intrinsic peacefulness is covered over and obstructed by greed, hatred, and delusion, but these coverings can eventually lift and this peacefulness can be accessed through training, through working with our minds. Trusting in our intrinsic peaceful nature encourages us to begin to look at our emotions with greater honesty and interest.

....

If your mind becomes firm like a rock

And no longer shakes

In a world where everything is shaking,

Your mind will be your greatest friend

And suffering will not come your way

—from the Therigatha

....

Dharma practice can be seen as an intervention. Without intervening, conditioning has the upper hand. What we have learned in the past, whether helpful or destructive, is the guiding force unless we explore the mind carefully. When a painful emotion is overwhelming, we so easily feel helpless, out of control, and at the mercy of our feelings. In the midst of a painful feeling, we can easily slip into reactivity and forget the possibility of wise and compassionate responsiveness.

There are countless wise responses, because there is no specific formula or recipe for responding wisely in the moment. Spontaneity and creativity become available when we are not lost in reactivity. A wise response is intuitive, not impulsive, and based on a well-trained mind.

A wise response is a response that alleviates rather than compounds suffering. Because emotions arise in the here and now, each moment is fresh and new. So there is always a chance to intervene. If we forget in one moment, this one, now, is one in which we can try again. This is very good news. Awareness is separate from our repetitive emotional patterns.

Difficult emotions function as wake-up calls. In their initial arising, they alert us that something is wrong—anger and rage may point to injustice, grief to wounds unhealed, and fear can be protective—but when left unattended, emotions such as these also have the capacity to mislead and deceive. After the emotion has ebbed, we are left with the results of our actions, and we are not always pleased by what we have done. Recognizing emotions as they are happening is an essential component of learning how to practice with emotional distress.

When we find a conversation provocative, when a family member is driving us crazy, or when we are about to hit the send button in response to an email that has bothered us, our first impulse may be to act unwisely. But when we are aware that the situation is giving rise to a painful emotion, we have the chance to recognize when an action is about to be motivated by emotional pain. In the awareness of this emotional pain, options for wise actions open up. One option is to exercise restraint. Restraint can manifest in many ways, perhaps as a pause before acting or stopping speaking midsentence. When we click the send button anyway or finish a misguided sentence, afterward realizing that doing so had not been such a great idea, we can form the intention to pause next time.

In pausing to observe, we interrupt the flow of the river of conditioning that pushes us downstream. We find ourselves freer to respond with authenticity and kindness. Over time, we find it easier to respond with wisdom and compassion, instead of out of habit. We can allow emotions such as rage, fear, and grief to call our attention to what needs it—injustice, unhealed emotional material, issues of safety—instead of simply allowing our emotions to afflict and torment us.

Emotions arise, out of our control. Once we are comfortable with that fact and stop the attempt to suppress or to judge them, our energies can be channeled in a more useful way. Instead of judging and resisting our experiences as if they should not be happening, we accept their existence. Acceptance makes it possible to see an emotion more clearly because we are not simply trying to get rid of it, and seeing clearly leads to a growing capacity to discern whether that emotion is wholesome or unwholesome and fragmented. Knowing that we don't know what will arise, we are free to meet this moment as it is. Although we don't have control, we do have the capacity to respond in a way that frees rather than binds.

When we are caught in the grip of a painful emotion, we also often experience delusion. It can seem as if the painful emotion is the entire world and matters more than anything else in the world. We fall into tunnel vision and lose our sense of connectedness with the joys and sorrows of others. When we are lost in our feelings, we lose perspective on the totality of life and forget that others exist. When we are in this state, the only people that really matter to us are ourselves and the person who elicited the emotion. The only set of circumstances that matter is the one that is causing us pain. We have narrowed ourselves into a very small world.

Practice invites us to expand our world to also include other aspects of here-and-now reality, as well as what is most predominant. One way to do that is by listening. Listen to whatever sounds are occurring. Listen to the sounds of the birds or of cars, to the creaking floorboards or the drumming of a driving rain. Listen to the silence. Listening in this way takes us out of tunnel vision and into a greater perspective.

Another wise response is finding a place of neutrality within the body, an area in the body that does not hurt and is not aching. Look for an area of the body that is neutral, perhaps even pleasant. To find a place of neutrality or pleasure can help steady and balance the mind.

Ajahn Maha Boowa says: "Whatever arises in the mind, if you don't get caught up in it but just stay with that sense of knowing, with the knowing that is separate from the event in your mind, then no matter what, that experience will pose no danger for you."

Getting caught up means reacting in an unwise way. There are three unwise reactions or habits of mind to be aware of: grasping, aversion, and identification. *Identification* here means taking an impermanent mental state as intrinsic to our nature. When we recognize these reactions as they occur, they don't have to lead us, and they begin to lose their power. We do not have to listen to, obey, or act in accordance with these unwise voices. We are able to sidestep an unwise reaction that would only compound our suffering.

As the Burmese teacher Sayadaw U Tejaniya points out, regarding every arising: "This is not yours, yet you are responsible for it." Both of these facts are true. In understanding both truths, we see it is possible to understand our emotional life differently and are able to live with greater peacefulness and grace.

"This is not yours" means that what arises is an aspect of nature. Because an emotion is nature, it cannot be personally claimed as being *me*, *mine*, or *myself*. The fear or anxiety, the anger, irritation, grief, jealousy, depression, insecurity, shame, or loneliness is nature, and not self. We can break the cycle of identification when we consider the difference between "I am anxious" and "anxiety is happening" or "sorrow is being known."

As practitioners, we learn to observe the stories arising in our minds without attaching to those stories. Over and over again, we bring our attention to the here and now, instead of dwelling in the narrative of past and future. This means sitting with the actuality of the pain felt within the body. This takes considerable training.

Emotion influences and skews thinking. Thinking feeds emotions. We tend to believe our thoughts most when we are upset, but it is during those times that we most need to question our thoughts, to not simply believe them to be completely accurate and true.

Through our practice, we can learn to meet our thoughts without claiming them as truths, or as me or mine. At the same time, we are the ones responsible for caring for our minds.

The text below, a dialogue between the Buddha and a practitioner named Kassapa, is from the Samyutta Nikaya and illustrates this understanding. (The comments in parentheses are my own.)

"Is suffering brought about by myself alone?" Kassapa asks the Buddha.

"No, Kassapa," the Buddha replies.

"Then by another?" *(Kassapa is asking: "If I am not to blame, is someone else to blame? If I am not at fault, someone else has got to be.")*

"No, Kassapa."

"Then by both together, myself and another?"

"No, Kassapa."

"Then is it brought about by chance?"

"No, Kassapa."

"Then is there no suffering?"

"No, Kassapa, it is not that there is no suffering, for there is suffering."

"Well then, perhaps you neither know nor see it." *(Kassapa may be getting a little sarcastic.)*

"It is not that I don't know suffering or don't see it. I know it well and see it."

"But to all my questions you have answered no—and yet you say you know suffering and see it. Please teach me about it."

"Kassapa, there are two wrong views. One says that oneself is the entire author of a deed and all consequent suffering one brings upon oneself and this is so from the beginning of time. The other says that it is deeds by others that bring about one's own suffering. You should avoid both these views, Kassapa. Here I teach another way. All deeds whether one's own or another's are conditioned by ignorance, and that is the origin of this whole mass of suffering. By ending that ignorance in yourself, and by way of yourself in others, wisdom comes into being and suffering eases."

In this short passage, the Buddha is pointing out that one way we misunderstand reality is by assuming that suffering is caused by oneself, that we ourselves are to blame for the suffering we are experiencing. The Buddha tells us that seeing suffering in this way is the wrong view and a source of suffering. It is worth noting that in holding this wrong view regarding ourselves we will also view the suffering of others as their own fault. This is the first wrong view that the Buddha calls our attention to in this teaching.

The second wrong view is that the deeds of others bring about our suffering. Of course, as we know, suffering is indeed triggered by someone or something. However, we experience it within ourselves and so can care for our pain within ourselves. To attribute it outwardly, to someone or something outside ourselves, is disempowering. It is so common to think that another person or situation must change in order for us to find peace. Believing this, we may not care for ourselves as well as we could and try to heal our own hearts. Instead, we hope someone else or something else will change. I haven't been all that successful with this approach myself. People don't seem inclined to cooperate with my sense of what they should do . . .

Ignorance is the culprit and awareness is the answer. Painful emotions arise dependent on conditions and pass away as conditions change. The emotions we experience are not unique. You might try an exercise. The next time there is an unbearable feeling, recognize that in this wide world of about seven billion people, someone, somewhere is experiencing exactly what you are experiencing. Most likely, a fair number of people are experiencing exactly what you are experiencing. Recognizing this is a way to lessen the sense of self and aloneness and to see our common experiences.

To recognize an emotion as an emotion is itself a wise response. This awareness of the truth of things, that an emotion is a mental state, offers a little bit of light. This light allows us to view the emotion wisely instead of through the eyes of delusion and ignorance. Awareness offers a pause. When we observe and accept, "Ah, anxiety is like this," for instance, we can experience an intimacy with the raw actuality of the experience instead of papering it over with thought.

Because all conditioned things are impermanent, painful emotions are subject to change. We practice sustaining the awareness that an emotion is happening here and now. There is the object—the painful emotion—and there is the knowing of the object. Because the pain is happening here and now, it is workable here and now. The story of self begins to ease and dissolve: how I was in the past, what happened when I previously experienced this, why it is this way now, given it is this way now it will be this way into the future . . . all of this is just the arising of thoughts that are inherently empty and occurring here and now.

Although we don't choose what arises, we have the chance again and again to see an arising as it is: impermanent and without ultimate substance. We cannot take an emotion out and show it to someone; it exists only in the mind. If the negativity is not compounded, it will wither on the vine, and natural intrinsic wisdom will emerge.

What arises arises because of conditions coming together. There is never just one condition; always, there are a multitude of conditions. Some we can see and some we cannot. Try to be aware of the confusion and sometimes panic that accompanies a painful emotion. Know that confusion and panic are mind states. We are easily confused by confusion, and we panic further in response, only to become further lost in reactivity. When we're lost in reactivity, it is easy to act in unwise ways or be paralyzed and unable to act when we need to.

When painful emotions arise, we tend to ask ourselves, "What did I do wrong, how can I fix this?" These questions may be useful, but we also have access to a meditative approach. We see that this emotion is happening because of a multitude of conditions coming together. The painful emotion is the result of these conditions.

Looking for the cause of a painful emotion through a narrative from the past is a psychological approach, and such an approach can be valuable. This is to be distinguished from a meditative approach. After all, becoming aware of the events from the past that have conditioned a painful emotion is certainly of value. Compassion comes more easily when we understand childhood experiences with greater sympathy. Good therapy can be invaluable. There is certainly a place for our narratives. But from the view of meditation, the cause of suffering can be found in the here and now. Meditative training involves looking to the here and now to resolve our problems.

The meditative approach may not come easily for those of us who have grown up in a psychologically sophisticated culture. But as we start to understand this and form the intention to try something new, the question becomes not "Why is this happening?" but "How am I relating to this that is happening?" or "What is the cause of suffering in the here and now?" Trying to figure out why we are feeling a particular way because of events in the past is a mental habit. The subtext of this question is that there is something wrong with what we are feeling. From a meditative view, the feeling is just a feeling and simply needs to be felt. We may often subtly hope that if we can figure out *why* this or that is happening, given experiences from our childhood, we won't have to experience the feeling anymore. Such a hope is actually a form of aversion and resistance, a mind state that feeds and prolongs rather than dissolving painful emotions. Many well-trained therapists understand this and can guide their patients toward this way of seeing that involves both a narrative and an in-the-moment perspective.

If we view an emotion as a problem, then of course that problem needs to be solved, and a solution found. But from a meditative perspective, feelings do not need solving. Painful feelings simply need our compassionate attention. They do not need to be analyzed or fixed, but rather experienced on a bodily level.

An interesting question to pose to ourselves is whether a painful feeling really is a problem or is it just very unpleasant? Rilke writes, "No feeling is final." Feelings are always in the process of change. In making space for unpleasantness, we don't add to or perpetuate the suffering. We are not feeding, rejecting, or resisting. We allow the feeling to be as it is. We practice relaxing and not grasping and are willing to experience the intensity of the unpleasantness. We see emotions as nature.

Again returning to U Tejaniya's words: "This is not yours and yet you are responsible for it." Who else can be responsible for torments of heart that I am experiencing other than me? Who will care for them if I do not? Of course, we can help and encourage one another when we are with someone who is suffering. It is a beautiful experience when we ourselves are touched by another's kindness. We can be receptive to the kindness and wisdom of others. We can help each other simply through offering moments of kindness. At the same time, we need to learn how to take care of our own emotional lives and recognize that it is possible to do so. Knowing we can care for and work with our emotional lives is a form of emotional maturity. Who can take care of us better than we can? We are the ones who know best what we are feeling and experiencing. We may want our loved ones to be psychic and to know what we are feeling, but of course they often do not know what we are experiencing.

Sayadaw U Tejaniya once asked me how much responsibility I took for my suffering. I answered, "Maybe 80 percent?" At the time of that meeting, I thought that percentage was pretty good. But his question awakened for me the ways in which I was not taking responsibility for the ways in which I suffered and was instead blaming others.

We practice turning toward, rather than away from, the painful emotions that arise. We are skilled in trying to pretend a painful emotion is not happening by denying it and distracting ourselves. Turning toward means seeing if we can pay more attention to the knowing of an emotion instead of giving all of our attention to the emotion itself, going right to the pain because it has such a loud voice. *Awareness of pain* is quite different. We practice turning to the safe place of awareness instead of dwelling in the very uncertain dimension of the painful emotion.

Discernment is seeing for ourselves which mental states are suffering and which are not, seeing wholesome states as whole and unwholesome states as fragmented. This is a way of being responsive to suffering.

Painful emotions can still trip up meditators who have been on this path for decades. Either emotions are not acknowledged as important, which makes it possible to dismiss the immensity of internal suffering by beings in this world, or emotions are overwhelming. Neither of these attitudes is liberating.

All of the ancient forms that the Buddha taught— sitting meditation, walking meditation, going on retreats, studying the Dharma— are deeply and immeasurably beneficial. And we also need to bring our practice with us into our personal hells in the midst of our everyday lives.

To attach to the idea that I will practice *at some later time* will limit our freedom forever. Later will always be some other time. It will never come. To turn toward the difficult, to turn toward suffering in the very midst of suffering is the only way to see through conditioning. It takes immense courage at times; it takes great patience and sustained loving kindness. But what other choice do we have, other than continuing to suffer?

Tertön Sogyal, a nineteenth-century Tibetan mystic, said: "I am not impressed by those who can turn the floor into the ceiling or fire into water." He saw the real miracle as someone able to liberate just one negative emotion.

5

Regret

....

One moment your life is a stone in you,

and the next, a star.

—*Rilke*

....

I AM DEVOTING AN ENTIRE chapter to the subject of regret because it is so often the domain of our sorrows. I have come to see, throughout my years of meeting with practitioners, that the narrative of regret, the stories we cling to and ruminate on, is actually another form of grief. If we were to grieve fully, perhaps we could relinquish our stories of regret and live more fully.

Regret is a tender topic, and we need courage and compassion to be able to fruitfully investigate it. If regret is unacknowledged and unexamined, the past oppresses the present, and life feels heavy and unworkable. To investigate where we are stuck in the past is to find a way to make peace with the past. We will never know inner freedom if we are not in harmony with the past.

The Tibetan poet-sage Milarepa said, "My religion is to live, and die, without regret."

Milarepa came by this aspiration through great sorrow. He trained as a sorcerer as a way to avenge his father's death, and he used his sorcery to kill many members of his extended family. Turning to the Dharma as a way to release his pain, he became a great sage.

Each of us is likely to share the aspiration to live without regret. But what does such an aspiration mean and how might such a thing be possible? To live life free from regret means to be awake and aware of each moment in as continuous a way as is possible. Those moments when we think we can take a break from awareness and space out are the moments in which our habits take over and regret creeps in. If we practice halfheartedly and think that we don't need to be aware in some moments, we are setting ourselves up for a life of unconsciousness, which we are sure to regret. Living our lives free from regret means valuing each moment as the best moment life has to offer.

Is there any moment other than now that is more worth being awake in? We would have to answer no to the question, given that now is the only moment in which life can be lived. There is nothing to be gained by looking forward to future events that seem better than this boring moment right now. This boring moment right now is our life, and everything else is just thought. When we make contact with the sparkling nature of right now, the specific content we encounter in this moment matters less. Ultimately, being present for whatever is going on is more important than whatever is going on.

To think that we might be able to die without regret is very beautiful, but dying without regret does not mean waiting until the time when we think we may be physically dying. It means to be awake here and now. In every moment of wakefulness, we are dying to the past. To be present, we have to let go of the past. This does not mean ignoring history. That would be foolish. How could we avoid repeating past mistakes if we do not remember them? We attend to the past in the here and now.

His Holiness the Dalai Lama says, "We cannot hope to die peacefully if our lives have been full of violence, or if our minds have mostly been agitated by emotions like anger, attachment, or fear. So if we wish to die well, we must learn how to live well: hoping for a peaceful death, we must cultivate peace in our mind, and in our way of life."

His Holiness is speaking of now, not some imaginary time in the future. Cultivating peace in our minds is called for right now. He is speaking to the importance of making our lives into our practice and practice into our lives. Milarepa's words pointed to his heartfelt desire to be of benefit in his life, to help rather than harm as he had in his past.

Milarepa's words are not an ideology, not a stance or posture. It is common to hear some politicians, for instance, say, "I regret nothing!" Such a statement is clearly a defense mechanism. I wish they would regret unwise actions or speech at least a little. It sometimes seems like those who should regret their actions do not, while those who have no need to, do. But what others do or don't do is less important than taking responsibility for our own mind states and freeing ourselves from regret.

We have all done regrettable things, sometimes deeply regrettable things. We delude ourselves to believe otherwise. To try to free ourselves from regret by making it into an ideology will surely lead to more regret. We need a heartfelt intention or resolution from which to investigate our lives.

Regret regarding past actions is on a continuum. It takes many forms, from neurotic regrets to the worst of harmful actions. Neurotic regrets often have to do with ideals of perfection. The meditator's path is not about trying to become perfect. It is a path that leads to inner freedom. I have found meditators to be some of the most idealistic people in the world. It makes sense that we would be; after all, we are aiming for the highest happiness. But when idealism is self-centered—as in "I" have to be perfect—it is debilitating and exhausting, certainly for ourselves but also for those around us upon whom we are projecting to our need for perfection. As the Zen teacher Shunryu Suzuki reminds us, practice is making one mistake after another.

Another neurotic regret is the wish or hope to be someone other than who we are. This wish is unattainable. In this practice, we are letting go of ideals of perfection in favor of the aspiration for inner freedom. Aiming for perfection can be seductive and compelling. Given that the society in which we live supports the idea that perfection is attainable, it can feel like our own personal fault if we are not. Yet each of us has our own unique contribution to make in this world and has our own way of expressing ourselves.

Here it's worth noting that there is a difference between harm and hurt. Harm is when we intentionally cause someone pain. Hurt is what happens in relationship, when more than one person is involved. Hurt is inevitable because of our differences. Of course, to apologize when we've hurt someone is skillful. But to hold the moments of hurt that occur in all relationships as equal to the times we have engaged in harmful actions is unwarranted.

Regret for harming others is authentic, not neurotic. When we have harmed others, sincere regret allows us to make restitution. We can use the opportunity to reaffirm our intention to try not to repeat those same actions in the future and to renew our vows of nonharm. We can recognize how essential it is to take care with our speech and our actions. Lack of care leads to regret because lack of awareness is the fertile soil of unskillful action. Using the guidelines of the five basic precepts—avoiding killing, stealing, harming others through misuse of our sexuality, unwise speech, and the misuse of intoxicants—are wise ways to avoid regret.

....

Like entrusting yourself to a brave person when greatly afraid, by entrusting yourself to the awakening mind, you will be swiftly liberated, even if you have made appalling errors.

—*The Buddha*

....

Regret often arises after the ending of a relationship, whether because of death or some other reason for separation. It can haunt, in the form of disturbing images of a loved one who has died, especially when we have been a caretaker. With heartbreak, images arise as well. Heartbreak because of the breakup of a relationship is a death, of course, but different from a physical death. It is a psychic death, the death of a dream, but often no less painful.

Unattended to, regret restricts, limits, hurts, and obstructs. Regret reinforces a sense of separation within, as well as in relationship to others. It is accompanied by other emotions such as anxiety, guilt, resignation, judgment, and blame, and it is based on the belief that I or someone else should have done things differently. If not explored and resolved, regret affects the here and now and life feels like a stone instead of a star. How can we understand that regret is not solid, like a stone? Understanding regret for what it is and what it is not can help return us to our star-like nature. Scientists say that our bodies are mostly made up of stardust—stardust makes up supposedly 97 percent of the mass of our bodies—so it doesn't seem so farfetched to think our lives can feel like stars, at least most of the time.

Regret is a mental state. The thoughts and sensations that make up what we call regret happen right here and right now. To truly be present, we are meeting with the residue of the past in each moment. No wonder that it can be so difficult to sit in meditation: we are sitting with this residue. We are meeting our conditioned patterns face to face. Meditating is not wallowing in this residue, though, but rather meeting whatever arises without adding any commentary. We meet these patterns with compassion and wisdom so that they can be seen and released.

We sit with our thoughts, emotions, and sensations, which is challenging at times. We are not just sitting with the lovely and the noble. As much as that might be our preference, we are also sitting with our demons right by our side. Awareness dissolves conditioning; the past is healed through being present. We cannot go back and fix the past, and we cannot live in an imaginary future. We can only live in the moment that is happening right now. As we keep sitting, our relationship to the past undergoes a profound change. This happens through our meeting thoughts and feelings about the past with inner balance here and now.

Awareness of regret is part of the process of awakening: in the process of awakening, we review our past intentions. We view our lives in terms of the intentions we had when we acted in the past. We come to see how often we've acted from deluded intentions, unwholesome intentions, intentions fueled by greed, aversion, and confusion—intentions that took one aspect but not the whole of a situation into account.

In meditation practice, we are changing our relationship to the past through not analyzing and reliving past events in the mind over and over again. Dwelling and ruminating are not meditation. Being present and open to learning: this is meditation.

Our practice is to be present. Learning from the past is absolutely necessary. No wisdom is possible without the intention to learn from the past, but we can learn from the past without being oppressed by the past or our relationship to it.

An unwise relationship to the past is often characterized by rumination, going over what has happened in the past again and again. I see this as a fruitless effort to change what has been. We unconsciously believe that if we think about things enough, we might change things from the way they in fact were. But thinking won't show us the way out. The hard work of practice is sitting and facing the pain itself, particularly as it manifests as tension and contraction in the body. We include the thoughts that arise as objects of meditation, instead of simply assuming those thoughts to be ultimately "accurate." When regret is predominant, acceptance, compassion, and loving kindness recede into the background.

Master Sheng Yen writes that the past is like empty space. Perhaps one thing he means by this is that the past, like space, is ungraspable. It is not that the past does not exist. Rather, the past exists *now*, in the reality of the present moment. We are always contending with the past here and now because the consequences from past actions manifest in the present.

Etty Hillesum wrote: "Everything has simply fallen away from me, leaving no trace, and I feel more receptive than ever before." The Buddha defined an awakened mind as a heart without residue, with no remainder. The "remainder" he was referring to is greed, hatred, and delusion. An awakened mind is free from the torments of heart, and our practice is the practice of leaving no trace.

During my first three-month-long silent retreat, a young teacher by the name of Krishna took me under her wing. I was twenty-four, and I was suffering in many ways. At one point, during a meeting with her, she said to me: "You will make many mistakes." I was a little bit surprised when she said this, but later, I saw her statement as a blessing.

Since that time, I surely have made mistakes, and I am surely not done making them. Krishna wasn't trying to be a fortuneteller, though. It was a silent retreat. It would have taken a lot of effort to make a lot of mistakes in that protected context. She just knew it is impossible not to make mistakes. She also knew that if I could be comfortable with the reality of mistakes, I could learn from them instead of getting stuck in shame.

When I make a mistake now, I try to atone as quickly as possible. If the mistake is verbal, I try to correct myself and ask for forgiveness as soon as I can. When someone criticizes me, I try to find a way to apologize even when I don't agree with that person's perception. I do not see these efforts as kowtowing or buckling under, but as a way of sustaining integrity. Master Sheng Yen writes: "I have been asked where there is anything in my life that I regret. I have had experiences where I did embarrassing things. I still do plenty of embarrassing things. But there is nothing I regret. When I make a mistake, I repent, accept responsibility, and keep going."

When I meet with practitioners who have lost someone significant in their lives, I sometimes see their grief manifesting as regret. Particularly when a loss has been complicated, regret can be predominant. It can be helpful to try to see regret as grief and to attend to regret as grief itself. The key is to try to loosen the narrative of regret, which is always the wish that we had acted differently than we did. It is not possible to go back and change our past actions now; we need to accept them. Because of the profound pain of pure grief, it often seems easier to dwell on the narrative of regret than to experience the grief lying underneath. Ultimately, however, it is not easier at all.

When stuck in a narrative, we remember only parts of a situation and highlight those parts, unaware that we are leaving out the rest of the story. The alternative to remaining stuck is practicing nongrasping, not fixating on thoughts that arise, thoughts that pull us into an alternate reality that didn't happen and is not actually happening. Thoughts having to do with regret are incredibly seductive, drawing us into a concocted universe that we fervently believe to be real. The medicine is meditation and wisdom, so that we can see in a different way, with a larger perspective.

A friend once told me he was suffering with profound regret that his mother died during the moment he stepped out to use the bathroom. He saw himself as not being good enough, as having left when he felt she needed him most. What he eventually came to realize, once his grief had abated, was that it was *her* life and her death. He recognized that the time of her death wasn't up to him.

Because death has been so medicalized in this culture and we are often geographically far from those we love as they are dying, I sometimes notice that impatience and the desire to control the time of death become part of the process for family and friends. The *metta* (loving kindness) phrase I have taught at such times, in relationship to the person dying, is this: "May you live as long as you need to." This phrase guides all of us in the direction of compassionate surrender.

Near the time of death, or in the midst of mortal danger, people sometimes report seeing the whole of their life flying before them. But what if that life review could happen now, in quite a natural way? If we sit long enough, reviewing our lives tends to happen organically without being generated by a threatening situation. The past can be resolved in the here and now through acceptance and understanding. As one Native American saying puts it: "When you are born, you cry and the world rejoices. Live so that when you die, the world cries and you rejoice."

One of the most wonderful gifts of the Dharma is the freedom it offers from all forms of preoccupation and defensiveness. We come to value openheartedness and understand that the best moment in one's life is always now. This is why there is a joy and lightness in those who have walked this path with diligence.

In the Buddha's time, someone asked why his disciples seemed so calm and radiant. The Buddha replied:

> They do not lament over the past.
> They do not hanker for things in the future.
> They maintain themselves on whatever comes.
> Therefore, they are serene.

The alternative to serene acceptance is, of course, the belief that we are more in control of conditions than we are. We may believe that we could have done things differently than we did. In fact, we could not have, because we did not. We acted or did not act on the wisdom—really, lack of wisdom—that was available to us at that time. It is as if we are looking back on an image of ourselves from the past and judging that image from this vantage point of greater wisdom in the present. We need to respect the power that conditioning held over our past actions. Conditioning has a tsunami-like power and needs to be respected as such.

This is not to deny or pretend that our decisions were somehow nobler than they were. Craving, ill will, and confusion surely often motivated our actions in the past. But with this perspective, we can make wiser choices now. As Maya Angelou understood, "I did then what I knew how to do. Now that I know better, I do better." This is true for us all. Because of awareness, we don't have to repeat the same mistakes, over and over again—we can make different ones! And we can align ourselves with the wisdom that is available to us now.

In a song, Bob Marley wrote, "Open your eyes and look within. Are you satisfied with the life you are living?" Awareness of regret rather than being lost in regret brings us to this potentially fruitful and creative question. Are we living now in a way we will not later regret?

In reflecting on this question, we can choose love instead of hatred, vulnerability instead of defensiveness, courage instead of contraction. We can look at our fears instead of being guided by them and later regretting the path not taken.

Through awareness, the burdens of the past can lift. We may continue to sometimes say that we wish we had or had not done this or that. It is human to feel this way, that we said or did something we now see as ill-advised. But we feel it fully, with simplicity of heart, and with the intention to continue to learn from our experiences. With the teachings guiding us, we might avoid involvement in situations we will later regret. Our responses are not complicated and burdensome, and we experience our lives as stars. To live and die free from regret, we meditate.

A disciple of the Buddha's named Cunda asked the Buddha: "What can be done for their disciples by a teacher who seeks their welfare and has compassion for them?" The Buddha replied: "Meditate, Cunda, do not delay, lest you later regret it. This is my message to you."

6

Loving Kindness and Compassion

....

Be kind, for all of us are fighting a big battle.

—Ian Maclaren

....

UNTIL WE GET TO KNOW someone well—and maybe not even then—it is impossible to know what losses a person has experienced and how profound the impact of those losses may be. Some experiences are so painful that it is not possible to talk about them or the ways they have affected us until considerable time has gone by or until causes and conditions support our speaking about them. With great traumas such as the collective experience of the Holocaust, we know that many survivors were not able to tell their children about what they had gone through, either for many years after or ever. One Polish man, an Auschwitz survivor named Marian Kolodziej, wasn't able to speak about his experiences until he had a stroke fifty years after his release from the camp. He finally "spoke" through his art, by drawing his terrible experiences.

My father is a good example of someone who couldn't talk about his past pain. Although he was a warm person and a loving father, he was also often angry and impatient. I felt protective of him, even when he was angry, because I resonated with his tenderness of heart. In a photograph of him from when he was a young teen, one can see the most sensitive of beings. We, his family, knew that he had been through his parents' divorce, after which he lived with his father. His father was mostly deaf and could speak and understand only Yiddish. My grandfather's job was to push a cart through the streets of New Haven, selling fruit. My father was his father's translator. It appeared to us—my mother and my sisters—that he had been impoverished, spiritually, emotionally, and monetarily, and isolated as a child, but we never really knew the details because he kept them to himself.

Many of us have been conditioned to be stoic in the face of pain. Of course, we know of our own losses, but perhaps we have been told we are too sensitive or should be over something at this point or just "need to let go."

Actually, rather than "let go," we need to *attend to* our own losses, as well as to the losses of others, with the utmost loving kindness (metta), compassion, and patience. In my many years of teaching, I've come to realize that a great amount of time must sometimes go by before people can share their most painful sorrows and attachments. Trust between a teacher and a practitioner can take time and may develop in fits and starts. At other times, trust arises immediately. Trust, like any other arising, is dependent on causes and conditions. I am aware when accompanying practitioners throughout their lives of practice that there may be much that is not said, cannot be said, even in an environment of trust. The secret sorrows of a person need love and ongoing trust to emerge and to be expressed, and even in such an environment they may not be shared. I have noticed that shame can prevent some practitioners from acknowledging long-standing addictions for many years. Secret addictions can continue in the very midst of a dedicated practice until they are brought into the fold.

Nietzsche uses a poignant and, to me, beautiful phrase: "your loneliest loneliness." I take this phrase as a pointer to the sense of separation we feel within ourselves—the many ways we are fragmented— as well as the disconnection we can experience with one another. The utmost gentleness is required to meet the intensity of loneliness in this world. When there is grief, we use the word *bereft* to describe ourselves. The word points to being deprived, being without what we used to have. We can also mourn what we have never had but have badly wanted, and we can ironically even mourn what we have. Such is the strange sense of separation between our realities and our psyches.

....

Though I'm in Kyoto,

when the cuckoo sings

I long for Kyoto.

—*Basho*

....

When we experience grief, whether immediate, long-standing, or as the haunting background in our lives, loving kindness and compassion are true allies. In training our minds, we find that we can turn toward our experiences with friendliness and compassion, instead of with reactivity and despair. Metta is unconditional and boundless goodwill that extends in all directions—toward our mind states, thoughts, body, and sense of self, as well as toward our dear ones, those we feel neutral or indifferent to, and even toward the difficult people in our lives. Through diligent and persevering practice, we aspire to leave no one out. Metta means nonabandonment. It means nonrejection, becoming ever more aware of our situation as a being in this world and, like all beings, desiring ease of well-being. We practice bringing a sense of friendliness to all things and all circumstances, including to our own painful emotions.

The practice of metta reminds us of our interconnectedness, which in turn further supports our metta practice. It is harder to nourish ill will toward that which isn't separate from us. Metta is a way of realigning the heart with the essential goodness that lies within us. When we practice metta, we are relearning what we have forgotten. We are reclaiming what we have cast aside—all of the unacceptable aspects of ourselves that have been rejected.

One version of the classical phrases in the formal practice of metta is this:

> May I be safe and protected.
> May I have mental happiness.
> May I have physical happiness.
> May I have ease of well-being.

These begin with "May I," which can sound like a supplication, a request, but actually, these phrases are not about wishing for what we do not already have. Metta practice is a practice of unlocking, reminding, and awakening. We drop metta in—to the body, the heart, and the mind—and then listen to the reverberations, trusting that those reverberations will echo in our daily lives.

The practice of metta is not an effort to convince ourselves of anything; it is not an effort to pretend, plead, or demand. It is tapping into what we really are, which is pure love itself.

Metta is not a feeling. Feelings fluctuate and are not dependable. To try to take refuge in a feeling is to try to find refuge in that which is impermanent. Rather, metta is an intention that guides our lives and warms whatever it shines upon. Metta is utterly dependable, once we have dedicated ourselves to practicing it, and access to metta becomes immediate. It is available and easily called forth once we are practiced in it. Goodheartedness becomes our default position, rather than just an accidental product of circumstance, an unpredictable feeling. Refuge in metta is a true refuge. It is always possible to rest in metta, and metta resets the course of our lives in a positive direction.

The practice of metta is, quite literally, a training. It develops our natural capacity to love, come what may; it enlarges our capacity to hold all things in our hearts, not abandoning ourselves and not abandoning one another. As we practice, our perception of the world shifts and we begin to see with eyes of metta. The pronouns of *you, me, us,* and *them* lose their prominent place.

The kind of love that the Buddha encouraged is not bound up with attachment. Letting go of attachment is not easy, but it means we practice offering metta unconditionally. "I'll love you *if/when...*" or "after *this/that*" is not metta. Metta is love independent of conditions.

Metta is always in the now and not some later point after what we don't like goes away. Metta practice is a way to bring space to our difficulties.

One of our difficulties is that most of us, at least sometimes, have to be with people we don't want to be with, whether physically or in the world of our minds. In the practice of metta, it is helpful not to focus on the person we find problematic, but instead to become aware of the mental states that arise in relationship to that person and to send metta to those mental states. Another practice is to bring to mind what offends or hurts us in relation to that person, the qualities that have harmed us in some way, and to send metta to those qualities themselves.

The phrase "May I and all beings be safe and protected" is interesting to look more deeply into because, of course, we know that there is no lasting safety to be found in conditions. Such lasting safety does not exist in the changing conditions of this world. All conditioned things are unpredictable. The Tibetan teacher Gampopa, who was Milarepa's closest student, pointed to this very directly, inviting us to consider how amazing it is to assume that after this out-breath, there will be another in-breath.

Metta is not a form of positive thinking. The metta phrases offer alternatives to fear in the midst of fear. It is a tremendously empowering and protective way to relate to conditions. When we are wishing ourselves well, our attention is focused on the phrases and on love instead of on fear. True safety, however, lies in not allowing thoughts and emotions to convince us that they are true. Only knowing infinite ungraspable spaciousness offers real refuge.

The Dharma is utterly consoling and comforting, just not in the ways we usually think of those terms. It is consoling in that it offers a way of facing what is—directly—without having to fight or flee or freeze. We find a way to live this life without cowering and without aggression. We find that we can hold our ground and that everything is workable. This discovery, this refuge, is wise view. This is the reliable refuge of wise view. We can find refuge in the here and now, knowing that we can depend upon our inner resources. This is deeply consoling.

In the midst of strong grief and shock, we have to prioritize ourselves. If you are someone who has tended to prioritize the needs of others before your own, it is a time to at least recognize one's own needs on par with those of others. If we don't, we won't be able to care for others in the way we would like, because of our own unresolved pain. My friend, Sarah, whom I mentioned earlier, ends each visit with me with a hug. While hugging, she says to me: "Take care of yourself. That way you will be able to take care of all beings."

One powerful way to take care when in the grip of grief is to practice metta while lying down, just before going to sleep. Sleep is affected by grief, and repeating the phrases a few times can soften the common experiences of anxiety, nightmares, and dread.

Compassion practice has a slightly different taste than metta and is the direct engagement with sorrow and pain. To bring compassion to grief or to any painful feeling means to first look at our immediate reaction. We might find that we judge our initial reaction as bad or wrong. If, instead, we could label our reaction simply as "painful," we could approach it with compassion instead of with judgment. We might be able to see our emotional difficulties and the emotional difficulties of others through the eyes of compassion, caring instead of condemning. The classical phrases for the practice of compassion are these:

May I care for this pain;

May I care for this sorrow.

Pain refers to actual physical pain and *sorrow* to emotional distress. We can also turn this phrase into a question: Is it possible to care for "this"?

What would it look like to care for this pain and sorrow instead of condemning it or turning away from it? Relating to pain in this way can seem so foreign, so alien, because our instinct is to get behind it and reinforce the pain or try to get rid of the feeling. As we know, those approaches don't work to alleviate suffering. Painful emotion wants to be felt 100 percent and attended to 100 percent. Then it will do what all phenomena do. It will change.

Compassion is linked with metta and yet has its own taste. Metta is friendliness extended toward all, in all directions, while compassion is targeted directly to pain. The two are mutually supportive. Metta makes it possible to be close to pain, as an ally, without being consumed by it, and compassion reaches out and extends care and attention.

Fundamentally, compassion is the willingness to acknowledge, open to, and experience pain. The experiencing is not just for the sake of experiencing but so that our relationship to pain can change. For pain to change, it first needs to be acknowledged. Compassion asks us to become very quiet and still. In this stillness, we listen deeply to ourselves and to one another. Instead of listening only to the inner voices of resistance and fear, we listen to the voices of tenderness and care as well.

With compassion, we summon up the willingness to inquire into the ways that we react because of our conditioning and habits of mind—with anger, fear, pity, denial, helplessness, and passivity—and learn wiser ways of responding.

We ask, what is my relationship to pain now? Not what has it been or what will it be, but what is my relationship to pain *right now*? Is there the capacity to care, the willingness to allow the heart to lovingly tremble? Is this possible here and now?

....

We evoke your name, Avalokiteshvara.

We aspire to learn your ways of listening in order to

help relieve the suffering in this world.

You know how to listen in order to understand.

We evoke your name in order to practice listening,

with all our attention and openheartedness.

We will sit and listen without any prejudice.

We will sit and listen without judging or reacting.

We will sit and listen in order to understand.

We will sit and listen so attentively that we will be able

to hear what is being said

as well as what is being left unsaid.

For we know that just by listening deeply

we already alleviate a great deal of pain and suffering.

—RECITATION FROM *Thich Nhat Hanh's Order of Interbeing,*

invoking Avalokiteshvara, the Bodhisattva of Compassion

....

Compassion invites us to cultivate the attitude of listening to pain where it is found and wherever it arises, with attention and open-heartedness. We are asked to listen without bias, judgment, or reactivity, and with the motivation to understand, to hear both the words themselves as well as the words beneath the words, that which cannot be said. We need to expose to ourselves our own secret sorrows, and we need to listen deeply to what cannot be said or expressed.

Deep listening in and of itself can be deeply healing and transformative. In the initial phases of practice, our narratives become visible to us. We see the stories we've told ourselves and lived with as if we are hearing them for the first time. To know our own story is necessary and beneficial. But if we keep telling ourselves the same story, repeating it in our minds over and over again, we limit our capacity to learn. To tell someone else our story, even just once, can be extraordinarily healing and beautiful, if whom we choose to tell is a compassionate listener.

Compassion includes contact, presence, sensitivity, and attunement. It is a tender sensing into, attuning ourselves with sensitivity to pain and to sorrow. In attuning, we oftentimes know what to do. When we don't know what to do, compassion may reduce the anxiety of assuming that we should always know what to do. A newfound confidence, a sense of capability, and self-trust arises in the midst of the experience of pain and releases us from our fear.

Metta and compassion go together. Metta sees and compassion listens. Both point us to what is needed. Sometimes simply deeply listening is needed. I was in Sri Lanka in 2004 just after the tsunami, hoping to be of some help. What became quickly obvious was that listening was what was called for, while offering anything else was overwhelming for those who had lost so much. Sometimes not needing to be needed is what is needed. At other times, action is clearly called for.

Compassion is the recognition of pain as being both personal and universal. We don't suffer in the same way or always to the same extent, but we all do suffer. Suffering is common to all and can bind us together instead of pulling us apart. Compassion honors this connectedness with all beings.

We share with one another fragility, impermanence, and vulnerability. This is not an exclusive club. As we know, people can be in the midst of the worst of conditions and yet know inner peace, and we can have the best of conditions and still be miserable.

When we open to and acknowledge pain, compassion springs forth naturally in response if it is not blocked by fear. We recognize that fear is fear, that my fear is like your fear, and your fear is like my fear. What else other than fear is similar between us? Our common bond is the desire to be at peace within ourselves.

As is so for metta, compassion too is boundless, measureless, and unconditional. The practice is to extend it to wherever pain is found. When we practice compassion, we begin to see where the edge of our compassion lies. For whom do we find it impossible to summon compassion? Toward those who are suffering? Toward oneself? Toward those who harm others? The boundless aspect of compassion practice means aiming toward universality, including all beings in our field of compassion. If we leave anyone out, we ourselves suffer. This is what the Dalai Lama calls wise selfishness.

In extending compassion toward ourselves, the key is to inquire into our relationship to pain. What happens when physical or emotional pain occurs? Do we reject or judge the pain? Are we afraid of it, resigned, hopeless, and despairing? Is it possible to care for this pain instead? "May I care for this pain, may I care for this sorrow. May I hold this pain with care."

Compassion is like a devoted parent caring for a sick child, with no fuss or drama and just a quiet attentiveness and willingness to do whatever is necessary. Or it is akin to the words of a friend of mine, who, when going through a cancer diagnosis and its subsequent treatment, invented this phrase of compassion for herself: "May I learn to gaze into the abyss of impermanence with quiet eyes."

Compassion means holding pain gently until it changes on its own and allowing the self-perceptions that limit and narrow our world to soften and drop away. This dropping away is deeply compassionate. Compassion means responding with care and concern to the reactions that arise such as shame, unworthiness, and fear. Compassion means letting go of our judgmental perceptions of others and allowing others to change in their own time, or not. It means daring to communicate when we resist doing so.

Being able to bear the pain that our loved ones and those most vulnerable in this world experience may be one of the most difficult challenges we face. We may feel that we could bear that pain if it were happening to ourselves, but the helplessness in watching others suffer without being able to relieve their pain is unbearable. It is worth remembering, however, that in a sense, their suffering *is* happening to us. Of course it is not the same suffering, but it still is pain. In learning how to respond to our own pain, energy is freed up and our capacity to listen to the pain of others becomes deeper and potentially more helpful when we are freer from self-centered thinking.

The way is not to try to power our way through, but instead to stop and to listen. When we are in the position of caring for others, is our care wholesome, or is it tinged with a sense of sacrifice? When service becomes sacrifice, investigation is called for. What would service without sacrifice look like? Spiritual idealism tends to backfire and leave a residue of resentment. On the other hand, what looks to others like sacrifice may well be joy. Only we ourselves can know which it is.

....

I dreamed and I saw that life was joy

I awoke and I saw that life was service

I acted and I saw that service was joy

—*Rabindranath Tagore*

....

We learn to trust the immensity of resources within ourselves. The path of peace calls us to allow the tight grasp of our sense of self to soften and dissolve. This is not a process of self-annihilation. It is a process of questioning whether the solid continuous sense of self is the deepest truth anyway or whether thoughts of a solid self are just thoughts.

In the practice, we are not replacing thoughts of self with thoughts of others instead. Rather, we are shifting to an openness and availability, to include what we have ignored—self, all beings, this moment, this life. We are becoming aware of the agendas we have for ourselves that are not to our own or anyone else's benefit.

Compassion toward those engaged in unskillful actions, actions that cause harm, is very difficult at first. Yet, we can reflect on the fact that beings acting in unskillful ways want happiness or at least relief from their suffering, just as we do. The problem is that as humans, we have found the worst ways possible to try to find some relief. In cultivating compassion, we try to see not just the cruelty present in causing harm, but the fear and ignorance as well. One thing that helps is the humility born of recognizing that if not for a different set of conditions, perhaps we ourselves would engage similarly.

A few years ago, I joined the Zen peacekeepers for their annual retreat in Auschwitz. One of the many discussions I participated in was an exploration into whether we ourselves could possibly be perpetrators. In looking honestly at this question for myself, I understood that if I had grown up in a racist family and joining in was the only way to get love, I don't know how I would have acted. Of course, I hope I wouldn't have been a perpetrator of genocide. I hope that something would have kept me from embracing such profoundly unwholesome family values, but I have to admit that I cannot be sure. What we can know is that in training our minds now, we at least have a chance of not aligning ourselves with the unwholesome and aligning with the wholesome instead.

When the Dalai Lama taught in New York City's Central Park some years ago, he named the many hardships his people had undergone in the devastation of Tibet. Then he said with a big smile: "But I'm pretty happy!" He explained that happiness is based in the force of compassion, that compassion is a unifying force that gives us strength. It allows us to feel at one with the boundlessness of life. He said: "If you want others to be happy: practice compassion. If you want to be happy yourself: practice compassion."

Ajahn Maha Boowa lays out for us where the path of compassion ultimately leads:

> Those who have reached full release from conventional realities of any sort don't assume themselves to be more special or worse than anyone else. For this reason, they don't demean even the tiniest of creatures. They regard them all as friends in suffering, birth, aging, illness, and death because the Dharma is something tender and gentle. Any mind in which it is found is completely gentle and can sympathize with every grain of sand, with living beings of every sort. There is nothing rigid or unyielding about it. Only the torments of heart are rigid and unyielding, proud, conceited, haughty, and vain. Once there is Dharma, there are none of these things. There is only the unvarying gentleness and tenderness of mercy and benevolence for the world at all times.

Along with sharing our fragility, we share the very same possibility of inner freedom and radiance. Compassion includes both sorrow and joy, both terror and beauty.

It points to the truth of nonseparation.

7

Relinquishing Grief

....

A grief and sadness—

the fishing line trembles

In the autumn breeze

—Buson

....

THE SATIPATTHANA SUTTA, THE SUTTA on the four founda-
tions of mindfulness, begins as follows:

This is a way, oh practitioners, for the purification of beings, for the
overcoming of sorrow and lamentation, for the dissolving of suffering
and grief, for walking a wise path, for the realization of awakening,
namely the four ways of being present.

This sutta is one of the most useful and beneficial of the teachings from the time of the Buddha, in which he directly addresses

grief, sorrow, and lamentation. How significant that given everything in this world he could speak about, the main subject of this fundamental discourse is finding a path out of grief.

Grief has a central place in the teachings because of the Buddha's emphasis on seeing into conditions as they are and understanding that all conditions are temporary. Through paying close attention to our experiences, we see ever more clearly into their instability. We see that no condition will last.

Loss is inevitable. Perhaps there will be many losses all at once; they will likely accumulate, as we get older. Perhaps we have already lost a great deal. As we get older, we lose more and more, but even children can be subjected to great losses. Grief has a central place in the teachings because of the universal experience of loss. The different manifestations of grief—sorrow, loneliness, regret, anger, despair—are all reactions to losing what we love.

We need to accept loss because we cannot really argue with its reality. In our practice we endeavor to understand loss and grief on deeper and deeper levels. It is easy to say that we know everything is impermanent, but if we really knew this in our heart of hearts, we would not try to cling as much as we do. If we truly recognized that loss applies to everyone and everything, we might try to love more and attach less. We might hold what we find dear to us as precious and cherishable and also open our hands more easily when it is time to let go.

Often we understand this intellectually, but not on a cellular level, and it is the cellular level that is transformative. The purpose of practice is to understand the laws of nature so deeply that we can find refuge in aligning ourselves with them instead of continuing to struggle against them. Practice brings about an understanding that is so deep that nonattachment becomes possible. We begin with the acceptance of loss and accept that, because of loss, we will experience reactions of grief and sorrow. We start to realize that this earth is soaked with human tears.

Grief brings sharp pangs of sorrow. Yet, along with sorrow, there is the backdrop of consciousness, the inner atmosphere that holds whatever arises, like the sky holds lightning. To be human is to experience the lightning strikes. Meditation can shift our experience so profoundly that grief arises and passes away, while the backdrop remains serene. Lightning strikes but the vast sky remains undisturbed. All beings have moments of being struck by grief. This is our human dilemma. Through our practice of meditation, access to the backdrop becomes possible.

There is a story about a Zen master who was seen crying after a dear friend died. When asked why he was crying—after all, he was a great Zen master and people thought he wasn't supposed to be sorrowful—he said that of course he was sorrowful, he had lost his dear friend. As I imagine what happened next, he got up and calmly made himself a cup of tea. In other words, he grieved fully without reservation, and then moved into the next moment as it was.

The point of the practice is not to override feelings, even painful ones. If we don't feel, we won't feel for others when they are deeply grieving. We won't be able to understand the losses of one another if we try to mute our own. Our aspiration is not to become stone buddhas, like the statues that can be found in gardens. Statues don't breathe, don't feel pain, and don't experience joy either. Trying to model ourselves after an idealized image denies our humanity.

Spiritual bypassing is a term used to describe meditators who try to "transcend" their pain by avoiding it, using meditative methods and teachings to do so. When we use the practice incorrectly in such a way, the practice and principles of Dharma are turned into weapons against oneself. Grief goes unacknowledged, and loss unfelt.

When we see very deeply into the very nature of life, grief is naturally relinquished. However, this is not to say that "we" relinquish grief through an act of will. We cannot abandon anything or anyone, including ourselves. And, grief resolves itself, without our needing to force change. In this way, we are in harmony and at peace within this world, even amid the sharp pangs of sorrow. Grief needs to be attended to, but it is not a problem to be solved. It is a natural reaction to loss.

As we look deeply into sorrow and become able and willing to explore it, we touch a kind of tenderness—an exquisite tenderness, the previous tenderness of grief. We can truly help one another, by accompanying each other through the terrain of grief. In the company of wise and compassionate friends, we can be companions to each other, offering safe refuge so that it is possible to open to this tenderness.

Once a year at the Cambridge Insight Meditation Center, I offer a bereavement ceremony, which is a space reserved to come together, bringing loss and grief into the meditation hall as a community. Some who come have experienced a loss within the last few days or weeks. Others come because of losses from decades ago. All are welcome. Sitting together and remembering our personal losses, with the awareness that all are present for the same purpose, to love and let go, is always powerful and healing.

In the moments when grief is experienced, we can open to the awareness that we, in that moment, are carrying it for everyone else, and that it is not just our own. We can tap into the awareness that grief is universal and that grief is not just "mine." In those moments of great grief, we are connecting to the grief of the world and are privileged to hold it for a while.

The Tibetan monk Gyalsé Tokmé Zangpo expresses this:

> When you are down and out, held in contempt, desperately ill, and emotionally crazed, don't lose heart. Take into you the suffering and negativity of all beings: this is the practice of a bodhisattva.

On silent meditation retreats, wholesome grieving typically and naturally occurs. This is because of spending the day in contemplation, without talking to anyone, in the silence of the retreat environment. In the stillness of the retreat, tender feelings arise. At the same time, we are supported by our fellow practitioners, as well as by the teachers of the retreat. Retreats are containers in which it is possible to heal the past. We heal the past in our personal lives by attending to images, thoughts, and bodily sensations, as they arise in the present moment. We attend to the residue in our lives with loving care. Not only are we attending to and healing our individual sorrows, we are also developing the strength to be able to engage with the suffering of this world, without turning away.

In the Assu (Tears) Sutta, the Buddha asks:

> What do you think, oh practitioners: Which is greater, the tears you have shed while transmigrating and wandering this long, long time—

crying and weeping from being joined with what is displeasing, being separated from what is pleasing—or the water in the four great oceans?

As we understand the Dharma taught to us by the Blessed One, this is the greater: the tears we have shed while transmigrating and wandering this long, long time—crying and weeping from being joined with what is displeasing, being separated from what is pleasing—not the water in the four great oceans.

For some years, I traveled to Myanmar in the winter. I practiced in monasteries there, supported nunneries and schools, and visited with friends and teachers. I have a close friend who lives in Yangon, and I am also close to her parents. When I am with her parents, who are very dear to me and quite old now, I sometimes think of a time when I was first introduced to the practice. I remember thinking that I didn't want to go through the process of my parents and other loved ones dying, again and again, lifetime after lifetime. This reflection on having to go through the loss of those I love time and time again in those early years motivated me when the practice was difficult to sustain.

As I pointed out earlier, when faced with a fresh loss, all of the losses from our past come together, emerge, and surface. Ruth L. Schwartz writes in a poem entitled "The Return": "This is what life does, as an act of great though often misunderstood kindness—it brings us over and over again to the same sorrows." As overwhelming as "what life does" may seem, experiencing accumulated losses offers the opportunity to let it all go, the most recent loss along with the most ancient. The letting-go process is tender, but when we grieve fully, residue from the past does not inevitably carry over into the future. Grief does not necessarily have to haunt and linger. Instead of believing that life consists of just one loss after another, that we simply accumulate losses throughout our lives, we understand that we can awaken and live in the amazing beauty of the here and now.

Consider this teaching from the Suttanipata:

Overcome your uncertainties and free yourself from dwelling on sorrow. If you delight in existence, you will become a guide to those who need you, revealing the path to many.

How does one free oneself from dwelling on sorrow? We would choose liberation if we could. We just don't know how to find it. One of our practice questions is how to work with grief in such a way as to be able to relinquish it. There are four approaches to keep in mind:

1. The practice of nondwelling
2. The practice of letting go of *me* and *mine*
3. The practice of gratitude
4. The practice of going into the very heart of the pain, and experiencing the pain as it is.

These four approaches allow us to release grief and delight in existence. To delight in existence is to delight in the here and now, the only moment in which life can be lived.

In families, I've always thought of the family member who meditates as the one who says: "Enough. I am not going to continue in the family lineage. I will honor the wholesome qualities that my family has given me access to, but I won't continue to share and pass down to others that which has been dysfunctional. I will live differently than I have been taught."

This kind of resolution offers access to another lineage, a lineage that can be called the lineage of those who have awakened out of greed, hatred, and delusion. This other lineage is one in which we are not imprisoned by our genetic and environmental background. Instead, we make the conscious choice to join the lineage of buddhas and bodhisattvas. We join those who are willing and ready to claim each one of us as their own. This is our true and noble heritage as human beings, to recognize our humanness, and at the same time, to open to the freedom that we already carry within.

One of my friends made me laugh at one point when I was in the midst of my multitude of losses by telling me he admired the full way in which I was grieving. To me, it felt like I was grieving as a two-year-old might, but to this friend, it was "full." Moreover, my friend associated me with joy throughout this time. He was not observing me from afar and commenting on my process. He was grieving with me, and so he could connect with both the grief and joy. Grief moving through a field of joy means letting go is happening along with the grief. It is not a matter of experiencing grief and then of letting go of that grief. We grieve and let go in the same moment. If we approach grief in this way, we do not build up emotional scar tissue. The heart hurts, but remains open.

During my time of intense grief, I was aware that I was free of self-judgment as to how I was grieving. This lack of self-judgment is one of the fruits of the practice. Over the years of working with so many practitioners, I've seen that self-judgment can be so oppressive, so toxic, as if there were a right or wrong way to grieve. There is no singular or perfect way to grieve. Relinquishing grief does not have to do with time. It takes as long as it takes. I'm sure I would have been overwhelmed by self-judgment as well, if not for the training of the practice. I just did not care how it looked or what other people thought. Coming to terms with loss was something I had to live through in my own way. The lack of self-judgment was one less burden on top of the pure raw experience of grief. I felt it as a moment-to-moment experience of hell without actually being "in" hell. Letting go of cultural expectations regarding how long the grieving process "should" take is letting go of an inwardly imposed burden, outwardly supported by the culture we live in, which dictates how we should be.

....

IT IS OBVIOUSLY POSITIVE AND healthy to grieve with others. If our past includes abandonment experiences, to grieve with others is a way to heal the old wound of having been emotionally abandoned. When friends are willing to stay close, no matter how wild or painful things are, the feelings of loneliness and isolation can ease. However, it is not always possible to have support when we are grieving. If you feel alone in your grief, please know you are not alone, whatever your situation in life might be. We are inherently connected and surrounded by our benefactors, whether those benefactors are physically present or not. Our benefactors are those who love us however we are.

The Swiss-born psychoanalyst Alice Miller coined the phrase "enlightened witness," referring to one who accompanies another who is experiencing pain. We can and must serve as enlightened witnesses for one another. Doing so has an immense impact on the person who is grieving and also on the one who witnesses. We can also be our own enlightened witness, in keeping with what Etty Hillesum writes: "You must remain your own witness, never shutting your eyes to reality." Whenever we are present and conscious with pain, without abandoning ourselves, wakefulness is witnessing. We bear witness to our own pain and allow the enlightened aspect of ourselves to keep watch over the fear and distress. Our perspective on grief either helps or hinders the process of grieving. Some ways of looking, held lightly, may help us to relate to our experiences with greater spaciousness and ease.

Events seem to conspire to bring our deepest dilemmas to the surface. In other words, our deepest karma, our deepest of wounds, can only expose itself, and thus resolve itself, when conditions support the revealing. This belief has been useful for me, as a way to summon the energy it takes to attend without "dwelling in" and as a way to understand my experiences. Grieving takes a huge amount of energy, and beliefs that support energy rather than deplete it are helpful.

In accompanying practitioners through the years as they have lost loved ones, I have noticed that it is common to experience great fatigue and sleepiness while sitting in meditation for some time after a great loss. We have to be very patient with ourselves if this occurs, no matter how long it lasts, and sit with others until we can sit on our own once again. It will pass, and we will return to our usual aliveness if we can be patient and give ourselves space to grieve.

All beings experience sorrow. In knowing a number of venerable practitioners, I have not known anyone who has not experienced sorrow. What is different for a skilled practitioner is not the arising of sorrow, but the perspective on it. Feeling is not itself a problem.

Grief is not a problem. Grasping is the problem and the source of suffering: grasping at the thought that whatever is causing the grief should not be happening. A skilled practitioner allows the sorrow to be as it is, while grounded in the here and now, without grasping, resisting, or nourishing the feeling. A person untrained in meditation may instinctually reject or justify their sorrow, which compounds the pain.

Relinquishing grief includes the recognition that loss is natural, and that in the fact of loss, there is grief. We try to remember that grief is a mind state, nothing more, and that it is possible to be aware of it and honor its natural lifespan—like everything else, this mind state is impermanent. The Buddha encouraged us to do what is possible in this life. He said that he would not ask us to do what is not possible. We are invited to relinquish this grief now, as well as all grief from the past—to release our ancient losses as well. However, even when we release it, grief doesn't instantly disappear. And releasing it in order to make it disappear never works. The invitation is to see the world from a vantage point different from that of loss and gain and the reactions that come in their wake.

Many people in my life have died, but three losses in particular are what I would call core deaths: my mother, my father, and one of my teachers. I miss them every day, and at the same time, I don't miss them at all. I think a reason I don't miss them is that these relationships were so resolved that only love and gratitude remain. Their love has taken root and has nourished my inner resources. My gratitude to my mother, my father, and my teacher has dissolved my grief.

In a study at the University of Minnesota, a biochemist named William Frey discovered that the neurochemicals in tears shed for emotional reasons are different than those in tears due to allergies, medications, or other purely physical causes. Moreover, he found that the stress hormones, such as cortisol, that build up in our bodies during emotional stress can actually be eliminated when we cry. In other words stress hormones come out in our tears. This is the reason that we generally feel better after crying. We are literally letting go, releasing sorrow and grief.

....

Crying out loud and weeping are great resources.
A nursing mother, all she does
is wait to hear her child.
Just a little beginning-whimper
and she's there.
Cry out. Do not be stolid and silent
with your pain. Lament,
and let the milk of loving flow into you.
The hard rain and the wind
are ways the cloud has
to take care of us.

—Rumi
....

When people cry on retreat, they are sometimes self-conscious, though crying in large meditation halls doesn't usually make much of a sound. Although the person crying may feel self-conscious, their expression of emotion is in fact good for the other meditators, who may come to feel soft and sympathetic. Of course, a yogi sitting nearby someone crying can feel concerned about the person who is crying, but it is rare that those listening feel judgmental. Often the sound of someone crying, in the silence of the meditation hall, points us to our own unresolved grief.

....

For the raindrop, joy is in entering the river—
Unbearable pain becomes its own cure.

Travel far enough into sorrow, tears turn to sighing;
In this way we learn how water can die into air.

When, after heavy rain, the storm clouds disperse,
Is it not that they've wept themselves clear to the end?

If you want to know the miracle, how wind can polish a mirror,
Look: the shining glass grows green in spring.

It's the rose's unfolding, Ghalib, that creates the desire to see—
In every color and circumstance, may the eyes be open for
     what comes.

—*Mirza Ghalib*
....

At the end of retreats, teachers and practitioners sometimes sit in a circle, coming out of the silence to share our experiences of the retreat together, before going home. While I was teaching a retreat in Cuba recently, we ended in just this way. One practitioner had been going through a particularly difficult time when she began the retreat, having been experiencing a series of painful events in her life, and cried quite a bit throughout the retreat. When it was her chance to talk in the sharing circle, she said: "I began this retreat in tears and I have cried much of the time I've been here. I am still crying now! But the taste of my tears is different from when I began this retreat. When I began, the taste of my tears was bitter; now the taste of my tears is sweet." She expressed, so well, the nature and the fruit of this practice. We continue to experience loss and grief, but it is transmuted into something so soft and so sweet.

The bitter turns sweet through the commitment to accompany ourselves as we experience grief. With any change in life, there is an emotional transition that takes place as well. If we miss the step of grieving fully, we also thwart the possibility of sweetness.

PART III

Joy

8

The "Feel Good" Gene

WE NOW ENTER INTO THE TERRAIN OF JOY.

We don't practice for the purpose of attempting to fix our-selves, and the practice does not have to do with self-improvement or becoming perfect. Inner freedom is far different and much more relaxing than perfection. We are engaged in training the mind as a way to access intrinsic peacefulness and a constantly available current of joy. I don't see joy as the opposite of grief, but as the current that runs underneath all of life. The question is how to access and swim in this current.

The Buddha taught that it is necessary for people to have a basic level of security in their lives, and that this security is a foundation for meditation. For those of us who live in relative ease, it behooves us to remember that improving worldly conditions for others is a powerful way of alleviating suffering, as well as paving the way for all who want to partake in dharma nourishment to be able to do so.

There are many scientific studies that point to the beneficial effects of a dedicated meditation practice. The one I like best has to do with what has been termed the "feel-good" gene. Recently, scientists have found that because of a genetic variation in the brain, some people are naturally less anxious, and thus happier, than other people are. Those who have this particular genetic variation find it easier to let go of past painful experiences. This genetic mutation produces higher levels of anandamide in the brain, which is a neurotransmitter that produces a sense of well-being. About 20 percent of the population is born with this particular genetic makeup. We either have it or we don't.

I was not born with this gene. And yet, the anxiety I began life with has completely eased. It is clear to me that the practice of meditation has made up for the absence of this genetic predisposition. I have observed this same shift in countless practitioners: the easing of anxiety and an increase in well-being. I have come to the conclusion that if we meditate with diligence and perseverance, it does not matter whether we were born with the feel-good gene or not. Knowing this inner sense of well-being is one of the imperatives of training our minds.

A dedicated practice makes it possible to go through profound pain without being endlessly lost in despair. Meditation allows us to keep our heads above water instead of being pulled underneath. I have a friend who has had a very deep and powerful practice for many years. In moving through an experience of profound loss, she confided in me that she had thoughts about wanting to die. Thoughts about wanting to die sometimes arise even for adept meditators. The difference between an adept meditator and one whose mind is not yet trained is that someone with a well-trained mind recognizes that a thought is just a thought, and so thoughts do not pick up steam and proliferate. We can have the worst and most tormenting of thoughts and, at the same time, realize that a thought is just a thought and not substantial. We can recognize thoughts as just thoughts and release them.

We practice being mindful of thinking, instead of spinning out and thinking about our thoughts. Without awareness, a thought-fragment turns into a paragraph, a paragraph turns into a page, a page turns into a chapter, and before too long, it has become a book. The theme of the book is suffering, without any relief in sight. In training our minds, we discover how to let go of thinking and how to not nourish and sustain the belief that our thoughts offer accurate information. Meditation gives us a way of working with the mind, instead of being overwhelmed, distracted, or tormented by our own thoughts and emotions.

The form of meditation best known is sitting meditation, and there is no doubt that sitting meditation is invaluable. In its essence, sitting upright and staying physically still is a posture of facing conditions as they are presenting themselves. The posture expresses an attitude of welcoming, accepting, embracing, and befriending whatever arises, in the forms of feelings, thoughts, and sensations. To sit in a meditative posture is to be present and still in the midst of agitation and anxiety. It is a stance of being open toward life as the forms of life express themselves in the present moment.

As we practice in the sitting posture over time, we come to experience the different levels of silence available, and we discover that inner silence is nutritive. In our daily sitting practice, we come to see that the longer we sit, the deeper the silence. The initial phase, when first sitting down, may be chaotic and busy. But as we just remain sitting, the mind calms down. If we can remain sitting for even longer, a great depth of silence becomes available.

Most Buddha statues are of the Buddha sitting in meditation. When people talk about meditating, they are usually thinking specifically of sitting meditation, rather than meditation itself regardless of posture. But to meditate means to practice ceaselessly, in every moment and in every posture. At the Cambridge Insight Meditation Center, we have a standing Buddha statue, to inspire standing meditation. We also have a statue of the Buddha lying down, in a room we call the Reclining Buddha Room. We have this statue as a model to inspire practitioners to practice while they are lying down. Some practitioners have to lie down because of a physical disability, and we all have to lie down sometimes when we are sick. Most of us will be lying down when we are about to die. It is well worth it to even out the postures, to be able to be awake and aware in all of them.

In this spirit, for years I have been trying to find a Buddha statue that is vacuuming. An even better model would be a statue of the Buddha conversing with someone difficult. We founded the Cambridge Insight Meditation Center to encourage the discipline of sitting, but also to encourage the understanding that our whole lives are our practice. At the time that the center opened, many practitioners were sitting residential retreats and then coming back home discombobulated, not understanding how to practice in the midst of a complex daily life. Retreats are, of course, immeasurably valuable. But to plan for the next time we can go on retreat and to forget the here and now is to negate the moment that we are in and miss the possibility of an immediacy of freedom. Valuing each moment of our life is crucial. Waiting to practice only when conditions are beneficial is to miss the point of meditation.

We learn many vital lessons while on retreats because of the simplicity and silence of the environment and because we are away from our everyday distractions and problems, but to mature in our practice, we need to take the situations we find ourselves in and relate to those situations with as much vigor and interest as we might when on retreat. It is possible to experience great peace in the retreat environment only to be overwhelmed after a retreat, especially when disturbing events happen in our daily lives.

All conditions in our lives are practice situations. Even meditative experiences come and go, and thus must be integrated into our daily life. The path of awakening is clearly complex. We can have beautiful and awakening meditative experiences and then panic when something painful and frightening occurs in our lives. We are complex beings, and although the practice itself is simple, the path itself has many twists and turns. A secluded environment is a beneficial condition, which helps in the cultivation of a calm and steady mind, but wisdom needs to be tested in our daily lives in the midst of both ordinary and difficult situations. We need to develop both steadiness and flexibility.

The Buddha taught the practice of *shamata vipassana*, or calm and investigation. The basic meditation instructions are to first develop calm and steadiness, and then to use this calm (*shamata*) and steadiness (*samadhi*) to inquire into the true nature of phenomena, which is that all conditions are limited, temporary, and empty. When these characteristics are clearly seen and accepted, we can treasure conditions without clinging to them. Calm and steadiness bring one kind of joy. Investigation brings about another.

Shamata practice is a way to train the mind to be calm and steady. When our experiences are more intense than we can meet directly, knowing that we have the option of steadying and collecting ourselves is essential. Awareness may not be up to the task of meeting the strength of conditioning in a given moment, and having a way to know how to calm ourselves is an essential component of the practice. Shamata practice allows us to develop enough inner joy to be able to meet unhappiness with inner balance, instead of simply being overwhelmed. It is a way to strengthen the heart so that we can meet all experiences with a sense of inner balance. To know that we can use our minds to calm the intensity of thoughts and feelings is an art that should not be undervalued. When difficult events occur, it is usually best to emphasize steadiness and collectedness. If our orientation truly is that whatever occurs is a practice opportunity, we will learn what we need to learn simply by remaining attentive and present.

We can relate to steadying the mind as a resetting. There are ways to do this other than sitting meditation. Some people find the same steadiness in martial arts or in engaging in an activity that they love. The great free-diver Natalia Molchanova found that diving was a way to reset: "Free diving is not only sport, it's a way to understand who we are. When we go down, if we don't think, we understand we are whole. We are one with the world. When we think, we are separate. We need to reset sometimes. Free diving helps do that." Sitting is like this too, but in addition to not requiring special equipment and an ocean of water, sitting and following the breath is a whole lot safer.

At the same time, steadiness and calmness are not the point of the practice. The point of the practice is alleviation of suffering in all of its forms, uncovering inner peacefulness, and liberating the heart. Using meditation as a sedative negates the Buddha's awakening.

Meditators often emphasize concentration more than is needed. Concentration is a support for wisdom. It is not enough on its own. This was a fundamental understanding in the Buddha's life. When the priority is the capacity to concentrate, when that concentration is disturbed one can be easily angered or upset. When concentration is viewed as a support, but only as a support and nothing more, when disturbances arise we look directly at the disturbance itself. We allow room and space and time to attend to the disturbance as it is expressing itself in the body/mind experience.

One of my students grew up in Argentina in the time when people were simply "disappeared"—taken away by the government in the middle of the night without any accounting of their whereabouts, never to be seen again. He had family and friends to whom this happened. Though the shock of his childhood continues to come and go within his psyche, he has found great peace in the practice. He understands that the point of the practice is not to escape into calm. He also understands that the calm he has discovered is healing and essential. We cannot make generalized pronouncements that one way of practice is the right one for everyone. Each of us has our own conditioning to work with, and thus we each need to find our own unique way into the practice.

Here, I'd like to use the example of taking anxiety as an object of meditation. One way to approach anxiety is by not paying attention to it, paying attention to an object such as the breath instead. In awareness of the breath, the anxiety is cushioned by calm. Its sharp edges dissipate. And, of course, the anxiety, along with reactivity to anxiety, will return. To look directly at anxiety itself is the development of wisdom. Looking directly at it, we begin to see its impermanent nature. Looking directly at it, we begin to see its impersonal and energetic nature. We see that awareness is separate from the experience of anxiety. In seeing in this way, we also have insight into the fact that anxiety is present because of the want or need to control that which is uncontrollable. In seeing the limitations of control, anxiety self-liberates. Wisdom is what brings lasting peace and inner freedom. Wisdom is seeing the laws of nature as they are.

An aspect of practice is to know what is skillful and when. Trying to fall asleep at night when anxiety is keeping us awake is usually not the time to look directly at the anxiety. It is usually much better to bring the attention, over and over again, to an object such as the breathing or the practice of metta. During the day, in times when there is an inner sense of steadiness and interest, to look directly at anxiety can be fruitful and liberating.

As we sit and dedicate ourselves to listening to the inner life, unexpected strong feelings can arise within the space and silence. The presence of an emotion we didn't know about can come as a surprise because of the tendency to harbor an expectation that the sitting practice should make us calm. Sitting meditation does cultivate calm, but it also offers the space and silence to allow the unconscious to become conscious. Sometimes calmness is not what shows up.

When we have developed a level of calm, we then use this calm and inner silence to look directly into the nature of things and to learn from experiences. This is difficult to do when we are caught in our thinking. We calm and steady the mind through finding an anchor to steady the mind on. Some usual anchors are the breathing, the body, or sound. Through sustaining the attention on this anchor, gradually thoughts begin to thin out and a greater degree of spaciousness is available.

So the practice of shamata vipassana is to first settle on a reliable anchor or primary meditative object to return to when we find the attention has wandered into habit and patterns of thinking and feeling. We encourage within ourselves the patience and perseverance to return to this primary object over and over again.

This object could be the breath, but it need not be. It could also be the sense of the whole body sitting or listening to sounds. We find whatever way we can to calm ourselves and to encourage inner balance, harmony, steadiness, and strength of heart. Doing so brings about an initial level of inner peacefulness. With this initial level of peacefulness, we can move toward the deepest of peace possible: a peace that is independent of conditions.

When there is some degree of reliable steadiness, the practice is then to begin to inquire. This is wisdom practice, vipassana, which means to see into the laws of nature, to illuminate all aspects in our lives. Seeing into life as it is needs the prelude of steadiness. Steadiness and calm allow us to dare to investigate because what we are investigating shakes the very ground on which we think we are standing. We need a sense of groundedness, which is what shamata and samadhi provide, to be able to stay steady and courageous within groundlessness.

To inquire means to open to all of the sense doors, instead of sustaining attention only on the anchor. We begin to venture out by broadening the field of awareness to include whatever is happening in the present moment. Instead of isolating the attention on one object, such as the breathing, we practice inclusivity. Whatever is happening is our meditative object. In this process of inquiry, we first learn to acknowledge and recognize the sensations, feelings, and mental states. Simply knowing that a mental state *is* a mental state is a huge leap of consciousness. Beginning to move into a conscious knowing is the beginning of waking ourselves up. With this conscious knowing, we can make different choices in our lives. If we don't know, we are embedded in past conditioning. Choice is not possible because conditioning is dictating our actions of thought, speech, and body.

After simply acknowledging, the second step is opening, allowing, and accepting. This is where love is necessary. Love is acceptance; acceptance is love. We love what is, whether what we are noticing is wholesome or unwholesome. If we can't get close enough to our experiences or don't allow and make space for what is seen, we won't be able to discern for ourselves what will perpetuate misery and what will bring greater peace, so this step is an essential one.

After that, the third step is one of discernment. We look at what has been accepted, to see whether it is to be encouraged or let go of. We look through the lens of nature, practicing nonidentification, nonresistance, and nonclinging.

Vipassana practice is wisdom practice. It is an openness to learning from experiences. Through it, we learn to bring a sense of curiosity to the experiences that occur in our lives. We begin to see the characteristics of phenomena, namely that all elements of life are transitory, insubstantial, and limited. This seeing is known as *insight*, seeing into the laws of nature so that we can live in harmony instead of in struggle. Insight is beyond intellect. If we just know intellectually, we won't be able to live what we know. To know in our hearts and in our bodies allows us to be in alignment with nature instead. In our alignment with nature, insight becomes possible—the kind of liberating insight necessary to know peace of mind.

A comic once published in the *New Yorker* illustrates what an insight is, quite succinctly. It pictures two gerbils side by side but alone in their respective cages, each of which has a wheel. The gerbil in one of the cages is pictured doing what gerbils do, which is to cycle around on the wheel in the cage, looking quite frenetic. The gerbil in the other cage is pictured lounging, completely relaxed, on the bottom of the wheel. The wheel has stopped moving because the gerbil has stopped running. The caption underneath the picture reads: "I had an epiphany." This relaxed and free gerbil realized that they didn't need to keep running around and around, keeping the wheel moving. This gerbil realized that they could stop. The gerbil, in its wisdom, exemplifies the kind of insight that emerges out of the practice of inquiry into the most important questions in our lives: We can stop. We can know our intrinsic peaceful nature.

We can know the true joy of the Buddha.

9

Pleasure and Joy

FEELING BETTER is not the end of the path, as essential as it is to cultivate.

The point of meditation is to discover a peace that cannot be disturbed by anything. It is to know the laws of nature and to live in alignment, in harmony, with those laws. Basically, we have to develop the strength and capacity to be able to look into discomfort and unpleasantness, without being overwhelmed.

There are so many delightful pleasures in this world—the pleasure of good friends, sexual intimacy, delicious food, beautiful music and art. There are the pleasures of a cool breeze when the weather is hot and a warm breeze when it's cold, the pleasures of connection, laughter, and appreciation of the lovely. Pleasant sounds, sights, smells, tastes, touches, thoughts, emotions—all these come through our sense doors: the eyes, ears, nose, tongue, the whole body, and the mind. While philosophers write volumes about consciousness, for our purposes, we can note that moments of consciousness occur quite simply when a sense object comes in contact with one of our sense doors. Consciousness causes us to experience phenomena as pleasant, unpleasant, or neutral.

Pleasure is a lovely aspect of being alive. There is an amoeba-like instinct to gravitate toward pleasure. Because we have a body and mind, pleasure is part of our experience, but when we try to get more out of pleasure than it can provide, we suffer because pleasurable experiences are fleeting. The path is not about repressing pleasurable experiences. It is about understanding that pleasure is not a solution to our dilemma of living in a world in which pleasure coexists with great pain.

As the Indian sage Nisargadatta Maharaj points out, "The desire for pleasure is the reflection of the timeless harmony within." In other words, the ache for *this* or *that* points to a deeper source of satisfaction. Pleasure reflects something deeper than itself. It is an echo of greater possibilities. Conscious moments of pleasurable experiences inform us that fulfillment and joy are possible. While pleasure is fleeting, the path offers the possibility of a deeper joy bubbling up from within. This joy is not a mere feeling. It is indefinable and ungraspable, available independent of circumstances.

Joy can be harder to understand and access than compassion. I have noticed that many people, particularly in Western cultures, find it easier to experience compassion in the face of pain than joy in the midst of the lovely. It seems especially difficult to experience empathic joy, joy for the good fortune of others. The reason may be that in the competitive culture we live in, comparing ourselves to others appears to be necessary, especially given the lack of a safety net for so many. What one person has, another person does not. It affects our Dharma understanding, causing the sense that there is a limited amount of joy to go around. We imagine that if someone else is joyful we will not be. This is actually not so.

In our pursuit of pleasure, we use a lot of energy trying to get more pleasure and then in trying to sustain it for as long as possible. One of our central meditative questions is whether that same energy can be used toward liberation. The Buddha said: "There are two kinds of happiness. There is that of an uncommitted life of pursuing sensual pleasure, and there is that of a committed life, one of going forth into greater inner freedom. Of these, the happiness of going forth is greater." "Going forth" means dedicating ourselves to the path of awakening.

If we try to make a pleasure last, it turns painful. Eating food that has a pleasant taste and texture is a good example. When we begin to eat something delicious, it tastes really good. If we continue to eat that same delicious food, we will eventually feel full. If we keep eating beyond that sense of fullness, focusing on the taste and sensations alone, we will get indigestion. Consuming food in this way causes self-judgment, because on some level we know we are substituting food for what we really need, which is dharma food. Dharma food satisfies the ache in the heart.

Another example is a physical sensation. Most of us enjoy the physical touch of another. It can be so pleasant and nice to be touched. However, if the person were to continue to stroke us in the same place and with the same pressure, we might start feeling a little bit annoyed. If longer, maybe the annoyance would turn into irritation or even anger. We might think or say, "Stop that, already!" If the stroking continued even then, it would begin to feel quite painful. What begins with pleasure ends with pain. The limitations of pleasure need to be acknowledged.

Pleasure is not dependable. Pleasure and pain are called "worldly winds." Both blow through our lives, coming and going. Just look at the pleasure of praise and the pain of being blamed. We like being praised and do not like being blamed, but no one can count on being praised all of the time. No one escapes blame. Even Mother Teresa and the Dalai Lama, two models of compassion in the world, receive both great blame as well as great praise. We can grow addicted to praise and feel highly affronted when criticized.

When we do get what we want, we feel a sense of relief for a short while. Sustained joy is not possible through pleasure itself, because of its transient nature. Yet pleasure can be an invitation into something deeper if we can remain awake as pleasure is occurring. This is why we don't deny it or judge it, even as we avoid the extremes of puritanism and hedonism. In the midst of the countless minor losses in a life, pleasures can soften the edges, which is a very good thing indeed.

Moments of pleasure cannot be accumulated. When situations in life are difficult, it doesn't matter how many pleasant experiences we have had in the past. Past moments of pleasure don't matter during these times because the painful ones displace them entirely. In the midst of a major loss, we often find that the ways we have attempted to find refuge are no longer reliable, and the temporary nature of pleasure becomes too painful to endure. When in great pain, pleasure lets us down. Where then can refuge be found? Only in keeping our hearts open and going directly into the heart of the pain. Going to the refrigerator will not be of help.

The problem is not pleasure itself but clinging, our futile efforts to make an experience of pleasure into something it cannot be, to make it permanent. It is not the fault of the object of pleasure, just as it not the fault of stones for not yielding water. This is simply the nature of objects, the nature of stones. Unconsciously, we expect lasting happiness from what is just an experience. We look for enduring satisfaction in people, things, situations, sensations, and ideas and neglect to turn our attention within.

During meditation retreats, we sit for hours during the day. In the retreat environment, the usual avenues of sensual satisfaction do not exist. Because of this seeming deprivation, practitioners sometimes lapse into inner fantasies, the only source of pleasure possible within the conditions of a retreat. Planning too can be seductive because it can be so pleasurable, and we don't even have to actually do the work of fulfilling the plan itself! The limitation of a fantasy is that we always awake and it's gone. At some point, we will come back into the here and now, no matter how far away we have been and no matter how long we have been able to keep a good story going. Even the best fantasy will end.

"Our practice is not to grasp anything, not to cling to anything," Ajahn Chah told a new monk. "But isn't it necessary to hold on to things sometimes?" the monk protested. "With the hands, yes, but not with the heart," Ajahn Chah replied. "When the heart grasps what is painful, it is like being bitten by a snake. And when it grasps what is pleasant, it is just grasping the tail of the snake: it only takes a little while longer for the head of the snake to come around and bite you."

Seeing clearly the limitations of the experience of pleasure removes the fever of clinging from it. We can still enjoy it, but free from clinging, it comes and goes without causing suffering. When we understand pleasure to be just pleasure, we remove the aches and itches and the desperate grasping of trying to make something out of it that it is not. Then we are able to remain awake instead of losing ourselves.

As a teacher, it is not uncommon for me to hear reports from practitioners about feelings of meaninglessness and nihilism, that one's life is not of such great value and just one long slog until we die. This is one reason there are such problems with addictions of all varieties, whatever ways we have of zoning out to avoid pain.

Dharma practice shifts the sense of no meaning and despair into great meaningfulness. As one saying goes, "The meaning of life is in the living of it." We can understand this for ourselves when we dedicate ourselves to living fully in the moment instead of concocting pleasurable stories about a future we cannot predict.

The Cambridge Insight Meditation Center is a daily life center, meaning that it is nonresidential. Practitioners go back to familiar environments of home and work after coming to the center to meditate and deepen their understanding of the Buddha's teachings. One practitioner reported that she drank a glass of wine each evening and was beginning to find drinking that one glass problematic. Most lay practitioners who are not alcoholics might have the opinion that that one drink per day is fine, and for some people, that may be so. This practitioner realized that she had begun to depend on that one glass of wine. What began as a choice had turned into a need. She saw that she was drinking the wine to make herself feel better.

Anything outside of ourselves that we use to make ourselves feel better needs to be questioned if we are serious about discovering true inner freedom. Anything that enslaves us is to be investigated, whatever it is and no matter how conventionally acceptable it is seen as by the culture at large. Appreciation of pleasure is far away from attachment. There is a difference between *wanting* (which is not a problem) and *needing to have* (which will lead to contraction). A practitioner needs to be guided by meditative culture, not conventional culture. In Buddhism, those ordained abide by particular rules and codes of conduct. Specific guidelines for lay practitioners are few. Our practice as lay practitioners is to live full lives and to free ourselves through investigation of the ordinary.

In this culture, we are told the mistruth, the myth, that we will find all of the meaning that we need through an intimate relationship, in getting the objects we want, or in finding a meaningful career. We are told we can find ultimate satisfaction where in fact it cannot be found.

The Zen teacher Kosho Uchiyama puts it this way: "When people speak about being unhappy and leading a meaningless or empty life, I wonder if it is not because they have taken it for granted that the meaning of their life is to be found simply in some sort of emotional pleasure. If you decide that only this sort of happiness constitutes the meaning of your life, then it only follows that you are going to find a hollowness in what you do, for there is just no such thing as never-ending pleasure."

Our practice is not to take even the smallest thing for granted, to look at everything with new and fresh eyes. We examine our experiences to find out for ourselves how things are, not based on what we are told, or think, or on how we think things should be. This perspective leads us to begin to look for joy where it can be found, and it becomes possible to find great joy and meaning in this life. We can fulfill our yearning through a deeper look into ourselves.

Clearly, practice is not always comfortable, and it is not always easy. It may well be downright unpleasant and extremely painful at times to make the commitment to remain awake from moment to moment, to live with ourselves full-time. In an article in a newspaper for the homeless, *Spare Change*, one person wrote so movingly about his experience of being homeless. He said that although he was living on the streets, he knew that true homelessness meant not feeling at home within himself.

Just as we need to look into pleasure, we need to look into pain as well, because pain is such a major part of the human experience. It's not that we need to look *for* pain—life will give us plenty—but we have to look deeply into it. One way to explore pain is in the sitting posture of meditation itself. In that context, when pain arises, we can, at times, choose to pause before immediately moving away from the pain. This doesn't mean being masochistic and gritting our teeth, but rather relaxing during this pause instead of acting on impulse. We practice gently meeting the pain and softening into the experience of it. Pausing in this way helps us to look at pain as it is and helps us to experience a freer relationship with the sensations that arise.

Sitting with pain is a delicate art because we are wired to push pain away. We tend to find that aversion and even desperation accompany pain. And yet, if we don't shift our posture automatically, we can begin to explore what pain really is and see that its true nature is insubstantial and impermanent. In our daily life, we can usually move immediately when we experience pain, so we don't usually come into as much contact with as much physical pain as we do when sitting still. When we are willing to be in contact, transformative understanding can arise. If we are not willing to look at pain as it is, we will experience life in a limited way, and we won't ever discover a true and reliable joy.

....

All happiness comes from awareness. The more we are conscious, the deeper the joy. Acceptance of pain, non-resistance, courage, and endurance, these open deep and perennial sources of real happiness, true bliss.

—*Nisargadatta Maharaj*

....

A new practitioner who came to sit at the Cambridge center some years ago experienced extreme physical pain on day one of a two-day retreat. She came back for the second day despite the pain of the first day, which I felt was quite courageous. By the end of the second day, she was still experiencing pain, and yet she was touching something underneath the pain as well. She had discovered a sense of peace and ease.

We can all touch this ease and peace in the practice. To whatever degree we do, it is worth it, because we also gain the willingness to be more fully with our experiences in life as they are. When we have more experience of observing without bias, we discover that a nourishing peace and current of joy becomes available. Etty Hillesum called it "the life current that never stops flowing in the depths."

We find that pleasure and pain are to be found in sensations, while joy and peace are found in awareness. A depth of practice develops through encouraging a continuity of awareness through the experience of both pleasure and pain. We gradually understand that we can learn from both.

As we examine both pleasure and pain, we realize the limitations of the senses and no longer see pleasure as an end in and of itself. As our attachment to pleasure lessens, an immensity of spaciousness becomes available. Joy is a deep acceptance, a deep opening and passion for life. We might wonder about the place of passion in the practice and assume there should not be any, but passion is necessary. Without passion, vitality is missing. Passion for life is different than attachment to the objects in life.

....

He who binds to himself a joy,
Does the winged life destroy.
But he who kisses the joy as it flies
Lives in eternity's sunrise.

—William Blake

....

We devote ourselves to a passion for life that is unconditioned, that is not dependent on conditions, that knows joy without a particular sense object. We find this passion when we are not looking for results from our meditative practice. It happens when there is no agenda and we genuinely let go and accept things as they are.

Ajahn Chah reminds us: "Do everything with a mind that lets go. Do not expect any praise or reward. If you let go a little, you will have a little peace. If you let go a lot, you will have a lot of peace. If you let go completely, you will know complete peace and freedom. Your struggles with the world will have come to an end."

....

The great sea has set me in motion,

set me adrift,

moving me like a weed in a river.

The sky and the strong wind

have moved the spirit inside me

till I am carried away

trembling with joy.

—*Uvavnuk, Inuit poet*

....

An essential inquiry for all meditators is whether inner freedom is more important than comfort. To really know inner freedom, we have to be willing to be uncomfortable on a regular basis. In my early years of practice, I wanted to go on long retreats. I did everything I could to afford and make time for them. At that time in my life, nothing was more meaningful to me, but I was also attached to my usual everyday life of intimate connections with family and friends. Each time I left, I battled internally with myself. I was leaving the familiar and the comfortable, and willingly choosing discomfort, loneliness, discipline, and the unknown. Choosing to leave home despite my attachments always proved to be tremendously rewarding.

I have traveled regularly to Myanmar with a friend whose health is quite fragile. Because the conditions in Myanmar can be basic and unpredictable regarding food safety and sanitation, she tends to get sick while she is there and is uncomfortable for much of her stay. Yet she returns year after year. The discomfort and illness she experiences have not stopped her from participating in experiences she finds meaningful.

The contemporary philosopher Simon Critchley speaks about "the compulsive happiness that plagues our culture." Perhaps meaning in life is actually more important than happiness, the meaning of knowing we are living our lives with awareness and moving in the direction of freeing the heart.

10

Don't-Know Mind

....

Don't-know mind is most intimate.

—Samu Sunim

....

"DON'T-KNOW MIND," A TERM USED in some Korean Buddhist traditions, is a practice as well as a realization. We practice remembering that we don't know and can't know what will happen in any moment beyond this one, and we practice being open to unexpected experiences, instead of living in our thoughts, assumptions, and descriptions. Describing our lives to ourselves and constantly commenting is very different from actually living life or letting life live itself.

At the same time, don't-know mind is a realization. We live don't-know mind from moment to moment and express openheartedness in all of our activities. In relinquishing the need we have to know what will happen in life before it happens, we open to joy. Everything we experience with awareness becomes new.

Don't-know mind is another word for joy, and *joy* is another word for wonder. Wonder is a sensing of the sacred and is not dependent on conditions and circumstances. Joy is a natural consequence of releasing and recognizing that conditions are largely out of our control. We practice reserving our judgments, willing to see in new ways. Don't-know mind is a mind that is spacious rather than narrow and confined. In this spaciousness is a tangible sense of gentleness. The willingness to inquire with a silent mind provides access to a life of wonder. Just before the Zen teacher Joko Beck died, she reportedly said: "This too is wonder."

....

Nothing in the world can one imagine beforehand,
not the least thing.
Everything is made up of so many unique particulars
that it cannot be foreseen.

—*Rainer Maria Rilke*

....

Don't-know mind, the mind of intimacy, is possible to bring as a practice into all situations. We listen, we open, and we pay attention. Wondrous is the mind that is willing to learn and to continue to learn, to see in new and liberating ways. We practice reserving the attempt to come to conclusions, avoiding assumptions and trying to sum things up.

Of course, what most of us truly don't know is when and how we will die. Of course, if we have a diagnosis that will likely be the death of us within a somewhat predictable time frame, we have a bit of a sense. But most of us do not know.

....

I can live with doubt and uncertainty and not knowing. I think it is much more interesting to live not knowing than to have answers that might be wrong. If we will only allow that, as we progress, we remain unsure, we will leave opportunities for alternatives. We will not become enthusiastic for the fact, the knowledge, the absolute truth of the day, but remain always uncertain. In order to make progress, one must leave the door to the unknown ajar.

—*Richard Feynman, physicist*

....

And the process of dying may be quite different from what we imagine. Three people whom I have sat with while they were dying all said some version of "This is not how I expected it to be," close to the time of their deaths. Each had an idea of what it would be like to die and confided those ideas to me with a combination of fear and hope, but the experience itself was clearly different than their expectations.

The first such person was a man I cared for as he was dying of lung cancer. Shortly before he went into a coma, he put his hand to his head and said, "I didn't expect this to be this way." Years later,

Morrie Schwartz, the subject of Mitch Albom's book *Tuesdays with Morrie*, asked me to be his teacher a number of years before he was diagnosed with ALS, and he continued to practice until his death in 1995. A short time before that, he scratched his head and said the same thing: "I never thought it would be like this." A few years ago, a longtime practitioner at Cambridge Insight Meditation Center was diagnosed with a brain disease and passed away a few months later. I met with him shortly before he died. He too said: "This isn't how I thought it would be." Even at the end of our lives, we hold assumptions about how things will be.

There is an apt *New Yorker* cartoon that illustrates our desire to always know what will happen next and the reality that we never will. The cartoon depicts two Zen monks sitting together, one older and one younger. The younger monk's face expresses deep disappointment. It is clear that he has just questioned the older monk, evidently his teacher, as to what to expect next. The older monk replies, with the cartoon captioned, "Nothing happens next. This is it."

This really is it. In practicing don't-know mind, we touch an inner sense of aliveness and vitality in the here and now instead of waiting for the next moment to be the moment in which what we are waiting for happens. In the spaciousness of nonexpectations, we open to life as it is.

At the same time, a sense of vision, of direction, is essential. There is a path leading to liberation and this path becomes visible through our ongoing dedication to the practice. Along the way, we can be guided by the wholesome—by loving kindness, honesty, nonattachment, and compassion—and we can listen attentively to the longings of the heart instead of following the bidding of the endless desires of the mind.

There is a great difference between ordinary attentiveness and meditative attentiveness. Ordinary attentiveness is based on our hopes and fears, like and dislikes. We are always picking and choosing what we want to be attentive to, based on our hopes to avoid the unpleasant and satisfy our desires. Meditative attentiveness is openhearted. We practice meditative attentiveness not only because of how we might benefit from that attentiveness, but also because we value a life of awareness. We recognize that the quality of attention paid to our lives is what matters most.

Many of us assume we know many things we don't actually know, in small daily life situations as well as in larger events. Years ago, before I knew anything about computers other than how to switch one on, I received a document that I was asked to review. The document that appeared in my inbox was not what I had expected. It was half of the document, or so I thought. I was sure that the person who sent the document had neglected to send the whole thing. When I asked the sender, she told me she had sent it in full, and asked me to scroll down. I thought, okay, I'll check again, but I know she only sent half of it. When I scrolled down, the missing half "magically" appeared. I hadn't known that it was necessary to scroll down!

Once on a retreat I was teaching, I received a note from a practitioner giving me advice in a judgmental tone about something I had said. The note was unsigned but I thought I knew who had written it, and my colleagues agreed with me. Later in the retreat, I met with the person who I thought had written it, and the note went unmentioned. At the end of the retreat, I received another note, apologizing for the first one. This note was signed, but not by the person I thought had written the original note. I was 100 percent mistaken.

All of us have had experiences like this. Sometimes we are lucky to get a reality check, and sometimes we are not. When our beliefs go unchecked, we endlessly carry assumptions around with us without examination. These assumptions become an unconscious part of how we perceive the world.

One of the shifts in consciousness that occur through a steady practice is that we stop over-focusing on conditions and thus stop relating to conditions as only either beneficial or harmful. Instead, we are open to learning from conditions as they present themselves, in both ordinary and provocative circumstances. We have a greater trust in awareness, that wisdom and compassion emerge out of intimacy and attention.

In the early '90s, I was in the Tokyo airport on a layover on my way from Boston to Myanmar, and while awaiting my flight, I noticed the Cambodian Buddhist teacher Maha Ghosananda sitting by a gate. He was hard to miss with his orange robes and kind face. I went to greet him and to offer water and sweets. He was quite old, and I felt protective of him because he was by himself. I asked him why he was traveling alone.

"Oh no," he replied. "I'm not alone. Wisdom and compassion are my companions."

If we think we already know what there is to know, it is difficult to see things in a new way. Everything seems dry, boring, sterile, and repetitive, but in reality, nothing is that way. Only our minds are, when awareness is absent. Being present is something we learn to love. It is an acquired taste. Being present in meditation is training ourselves in sustaining wakefulness, whether the content of the moment is pleasant or not.

We can apply don't-know mind to our relationships. One common habit of mind in relationship to others is to judge and evaluate according to our views and opinions about how others should behave (as one saying goes: it's easier to see an ant on another's nose than a yak on your own). However, we can try seeing differently and with greater understanding and compassion. As Rumi wrote: "Half of any person is wrong and weak and off the path. Half! The other half is dancing and swimming and flying in the invisible joy."

At the Cambridge Insight Meditation Center, we used to have a brochure with the image of a Buddha whose nose had broken off. It was a photograph of a statue in Sarnath, India, in what was once a deer park where the Buddha taught his first disciples. I was able to visit the statue and see it for myself. We don't use the image anymore, but while we did, I liked it very much. To me, it signified the reality of our inherent peaceful nature, as well as our humanness. It reminded me that we all have the same nature as the Buddha's, and at the same time, we are all a bit broken. It is the difference between practice for the sake of perfection and practice in the service of liberation.

Linking our motivations to the motivations of others can be a way to perceive the behavior of others in more spacious and compassionate ways. We do the most foolish of things, at times. Why do we do what we do? We act as we do in efforts to relieve anxiety and fear, and to find peace and happiness. This motivation is the same for others as well.

So often, we assume we know the intentions of others, but we really cannot truly know them with certainty unless they tell us, and maybe not even then. We can only know our own intentions, and even that is difficult. It requires a great degree of awareness, honesty, and interest to be conscious of our own intentions, particularly given that our intentions change from moment to moment. We may begin a certain interaction with one intention, thinking it will carry us through, and then find that it doesn't. We need to be aware consistently, to catch sight of our intentions shifting from skillful to unskillful, and back and forth between the two.

What we can see are actions—our own and those of others. Our seeing can be a way of tracing back what intention motivated our own actions, and this kind of self-knowledge is invaluable. When it comes to others, we can only see actions and respond accordingly. When we forget the basic fact that we can never fully know another's intentions, we tend to build stories about that person, speculating and making assumptions about their actions, based on our own concoctions.

Accordingly, one way we can practice don't-know mind lies in the effort to be aware of presuming we know someone more than they know themselves. A person is an entire universe, mysterious and impossible to completely know. Understanding that we cannot fully know what is happening in another's mind frees up immense energy. This awareness opens up the possibility of relating to one another in fresh and immediate ways, rather than being confined by our biases.

In her book *Number Our Days,* Barbara Myerhoff quotes Shmuel Goldman:

I have a friend. A woman I already know many years. One day she is mad at me. From nowhere it comes. I have insulted her, she tells me. How? I don't know. Why don't I know? Because I don't know her. She surprised me. That's good. That is how it should be. You cannot tell someone, "I know you." People jump around. They are like a ball. Rubbery they bounce. A ball cannot be long in one place. Rubbery, it must jump. So what do you do to keep a person from jumping? The same as with a ball. You take a pin and stick it in, make a little hole, it goes flat. When you tell someone, "I know you" you put a little pin in. So what should you do? Leave them be. Don't try to make them stand still for your convenience. You don't ever know them. Let people surprise you. This likewise you can do concerning yourself. All this I didn't read in any book. It is my own invention.

Earlier I mentioned a beloved member of the Cambridge Insight Meditation Center who died of a brain disease. What was so striking about seeing him between his diagnosis and the time of his death is how much he remained "himself." In fact, he became more "himself." He had practiced generosity and kindness during his many years at the center, and in those short few months between his diagnosis and his death, those close to him saw him distilled down to these qualities of heart. Nothing was left of him other than his pure-heartedness. All of the ordinary fears and neuroses were gone, replaced by pure love.

Even in relationship to ourselves, we can practice don't-know mind. When we observe our own mental habits, we might see that worry is a predominant theme, particularly in relationship to ourselves: *Am I good enough? Am I better or worse than this or that person? Am I a good meditator, a bad meditator, a good parent, child, friend, lawyer, retiree?* We evaluate, we assess, we worry, we compare. On another day, the content we are assessing can be completely different. Seeing these patterns assert themselves and vanish allows them to drop away. This seeing is a practice of don't-know mind. We observe our fickle minds.

What we call "myself" is a collection of habits and patterns. We assume various identities, which actually change from moment to moment: *I am someone who never* . . . or *always* . . . or *is like this* or *like that*. Practicing don't-know mind is exploring the ways we've identified with patterns and habits as the essence of who we are, seeing ideas and beliefs about ourselves that we cling to. Practice means seeing and recognizing patterns and habits, and noticing the huge leap we often make from a pattern to an identity.

Of course, patterns and habits of mind are deeply conditioned. We have unconsciously practiced them over the years. This has empowered them. But we need not be intimidated by what, after all, is just a thought. The arising of the same pattern, time after time, is not in and of itself our concern. The arising of a pattern is out of our control. Our concern is to not cause harm to one another. It doesn't matter how often a pattern arises, as long as we see it. Attention and wisdom loosen the pattern. The practice is to continue to observe, open, and release, allowing awareness to unstick what has been stuck. Realizing the nature of things directly requires releasing how we think things are, so that we can discover how things really are.

Don't-know mind can also be applied to situations and circumstances. When anything happens in our life, we tend to see it through the lens of good or bad. Over time, however, what seemed like good luck does not always prove itself to be so. Of course, sometimes an event is truly good luck, as in winning the lottery, but even then, life can be more complicated than expected: one study about lottery winners found that after the initial thrill of winning, lottery winners were no happier than recent car crash victims.

When we find ourselves in what is conventionally called a good situation, of course we want it to last. But if we are carried away by positive experiences—being praised, approved of, succeeding, and gaining what we think we want—the practice is unlikely to support us through the difficult times that will inevitably come later. We have to practice on both ends, in times that are positive and in times that are problematic. This means holding concepts—especially *good* and *bad*—very lightly.

If we keep our minds open when positive events occur, we are less likely to tense up when difficult events come. If we don't lock on to a given success, we will be more able to remain openhearted when we fail. With openheartedness, we find ourselves in direct touch with life as it unfolds from moment to moment, instead of as caught up in beliefs and concepts. If we are not attached to praise, we will not suffer as much when blame comes our way.

One of the benefits of an established practice is that because we see everything that happens as a practice opportunity, our bad luck becomes the practice as well. Although we would never wish our difficulties on anyone else, we can actually experience gratitude for the difficult. After the initial shock wears off, we recognize that certain qualities of heart have had to emerge to meet the difficult, and we cherish these qualities. We realize that our quality of life and of consciousness has changed for the better because of having had to meet unwanted circumstances with wisdom and compassion.

If we see unfortunate events as practice, the invaluable and hard-won gifts of patience, empathy, and humility become mature. These inner qualities of heart cannot be lost or taken away by anyone or anything.

In *The Trauma of Everyday Life,* Mark Epstein notes that as a therapist, he sees the rush to normalize when painful events occur and reflects that this effort to return to normal closes the heart. Our conditioning has taught us that we should not feel as we do—a very painful lesson given that the arising of feelings is out of our control. Because of this, meditation practice can be a surprise. We generally feel more acutely and with greater poignancy rather than less. At the same time, feelings pass more quickly, because we are not feeding them. We find ourselves open to the next moment more easily.

It is wisdom to know the difference between mere knowledge and the kind of deeper understanding that can liberate the heart. Distinguishing between accumulated facts and information and intuitive inherent wisdom is essential. Of course, we need knowledge and information. But in this era of social media we are drowning in information. Hearing and studying the Buddha's teachings offer an essential knowledge of key principles, and that knowledge is indeed valuable. According to the teachings, there are three kinds of wisdom: heard wisdom (knowledge that comes through listening and reading), wisdom that is gained through reflecting on the principles of the Dharma in relationship to our daily lives, and experiential wisdom, wisdom that is practiced and lived. This last kind of wisdom leads to a true inner transformation.

A meditative approach is to pause, stop, and be still. If we can be aware of our fixed ideas—about ourselves, about other people, about this world—those fixed ideas can begin to dissolve. As we relax our beliefs in concepts, we find ourselves more available, less preoccupied, and naturally responsive. We experience life in a fresh way, which allows our reactions to be fully experienced as well as fully released. New pathways open, and creativity emerges that we did not even know was available.

When we question our familiar ways of being in life, we may initially feel the loss of the old and familiar. What is the new? Where can we rest now, without our fixed ideas and attachment to assumptions to rely upon? The familiar points of orientation are gone and the new has not yet appeared.

In the past, we may have tried to maximize pleasurable experiences and minimize unpleasant ones. Maybe we were oriented toward wanting others to see us in particular ways. Maybe we wanted something specifically and wanted to get rid of something else, the direction of our lives pointed toward getting or getting rid of. When our orientation changes, we can feel shaky because we do not yet know the new. Is what we were pursuing really worth pursuing?

We do not need to have the answers to these kinds of questions. It is a relief to let go of the need to know. In fact, it is better not to think we need to answer these kinds of questions and to allow authentic responses to arise on their own. Our orientation shifts from closed to open, perhaps open within the shakiness until we find a true place of rest and trust within the heart.

Directly understanding the nature of things requires releasing the old, even if the old means the moment that came just before this one. We discover a selfless silence—hidden within the thicket of agendas and concepts—as reactivity eases and a natural responsiveness flows forth. When we are aware of fixations, they gradually and eventually dissolve. It's worth noting that when we find ourselves stuck on one perception or theme or emotion, we can become unhappy or happy. We are unhappy when we think to ourselves: *Here I am stuck again.*

This word "again" is always a problem because nothing is actually ever happening *again*—it is all only ever happening now. Alternatively, we could be happy to see the habits and patterns that have been unconscious up until now, remembering that the seeing itself means that a loosening is already in process. Seeing in this way allows for allowing everything to come and for everything to be released.

As practitioners, we are opening to this life, with its great beauties and unpredictable sorrows. If we assume we already know, it is impossible to see in a new way.

The Buddha called us to the practice with the (Pali) word *ehipasiko*. *Ehipasiko* means to come and see for ourselves how things are underneath appearances. It is a call to practice and to realize don't-know mind, this mind that is (as Samu Sunim put it) "most intimate."

II

From Hope to Faith

MOST OF US WOULD NOT begin to meditate at all, if not for hope. We hope for relief from our pain. We hope for peace of mind. We hope for transformation and transcendence. We hope for nirvana. Initially, and usually for quite a long time, hope is what motivates us to practice. As practice matures, however, hope is not enough to sustain us, but if we can continue to practice through the ups and downs, hope turns into trust. Hope turns into trusting with unshakable confidence in our own capacities, the truths of the teachings, and the lawfulness of phenomena. The path itself turns hope into trust.

Hope is the desire that something change for the better at some specific or undetermined point in the future. We hope that our desires will be satisfied. We hope events will turn out for the best and that conditions will be better than the way they are right now. Hope is the yearning that a situation will get better. When it does not, the result is disappointment, at the very least. In the wake of hope, when our hopes are dashed or not fulfilled, comes discouragement, fear, anxiety, worry, despair, resistance, resentment, and the effort to control. Clinging to hopes, agendas, and expectations can make our suffering and the suffering of those around us worse.

When conditions are momentarily as we want them to be, we hope they won't change. We hope they will remain as they are. We hope the situation we are in will be the one thing not subject to the law of impermanence.

Our hopes can be vague and general or extremely specific, involving our personal and shared stories of being in this world together, such as world peace or at least not blowing one another up. The content can be anything, in the realm of health, work, politics, relationships. It can have to do with meditation: *I hope to be a better meditator in the future.* Our hopes can be very small and narrow or big and noble. We tend to have both kinds of hope, the very small and the very big.

Hope is important, because it points to our aspirations and toward a vision of how life could be. Hope is necessary in a life until it can be replaced by trust. It can make bearable moments that would otherwise be unbearable, and it can help us survive and endure until conditions change. Turning hope into faith does not mean taking hope away. We would never want to take anyone else's hope away from them. It is natural to dream about a better life. Hope needs to be respected and honored.

Hope reminds us that, when we or those we love are very sick, or in the process of dying, we or they are still very much alive. Leo Tolstoy's novella *The Death of Ivan Ilyich,* about a man who is dying at home with family and friends, illuminates this theme. Tolstoy makes very clear that it is as if this man—this husband, father, and friend—

is already dead, even as he moves through the process of dying. His family and friends treat him as if he is already gone and invisible to them. They fear him because they fear being reminded (as the Buddha was) of the realities of old age, sickness, and death. Such stories remind us of the temporary nature of this body and mind. When our body or the body of someone we love begins to break down, if we fear rather than accept this natural process, we disconnect as a way to prepare for their loss. This is rarely skillful. I have been with many people through their process of dying; what is always so clear is that each person, even if in a coma, has been vitally alive until they were not.

One of my nieces had a very painful time when she was in junior high school. Everyone at school would come to her with their problems, and she would do her best to try to resolve them. This was not an easy position to be in. Sometimes after a hard day, her mom would say to her: "Tomorrow's another day," which would lift her spirits. She had another chance to do things differently "tomorrow." Such a simple thing, yet it made a huge difference to her. To hear these words, from her mom, enabled her to go back to school the next day. This hope for a better tomorrow helped her to endure the mental state she was experiencing. Even if "tomorrow" is a concept, it is a useful and necessary concept to help us to envision a better way forward on another day.

As we continue in our practice, however, hope begins to mean less to us. We begin to see into hope and the idea of tomorrow as a concept. Always, hoping means looking to the future for fulfillment, instead of to the here and now. As our practice matures, we come increasingly to value being here, now, present and alive within our lives without dependency on an imaginary future. We get a glimpse into the fact that the path is guiding us toward something much deeper and more reliable than hope. Gradually, through practicing, and through immersion in the teachings, which become ever more tangible and realizable, we begin to see the limitations, fragility, and instability of hope. We begin to place our trust in life lived now.

The environmentalist Paul Kingsnorth has this to say about hope:

Whenever I hear the word *hope* these days, I reach for my whiskey bottle. It seems to me to be such a futile thing. What does it mean? What are we hoping for? And why are we reduced to something so desperate? Surely we only hope when we are powerless.

Thus free from hope, Kingsworth is that rare global warming activist who is not burned out.

Are we powerless? In terms of making conditions the way we want them to be, in one sense we often are. And because of this powerlessness, our practice is to surrender. So very much is out of our control. But from the perspective of the practice, we are also far from powerless. We discover this when our hopes shift to confidence and faith and we are no longer caught in the cycle of hope and fear. We begin to see beyond hope and fear. The opposite of hope is despair, and the opposite of faith is doubt. We begin to realize that what our doubt tells us is not necessarily true. We can investigate our doubts and attend to doubt as a mental state that comes and goes, realizing that we can doubt our doubts instead of placing our trust in our doubts.

As hope becomes less important, we are able to be more present and love the present moment. We can use the energies that went into hoping for an easier, lighter future for the purpose of awakening right now and uncovering the joy that is always available. Hope fragments our experiences in life. Because a portion of our energy is caught by our thoughts about the future, when we are less invested in thoughts about the future we are freed to bring a curiosity to that which is happening now, to see more clearly the causes of happiness and suffering. Everything is only happening now. Believing too rigidly in our thoughts deludes us into thinking that the future is something controllable. So we practice redirecting ourselves away from this delusion and toward intrinsic wisdom and inner freedom, which can only be realized now.

Trust, or faith and confidence, is different than hope. The Pali word for faith is *saddha*, which means "to hand our hearts over." The kind of faith the Buddha favored and taught was what he called *verified faith,* trusting in that which can be verified within our own experiences instead of relying on the words of someone else. Many of us just beginning this path appreciate the encouragement to test and question the teachings instead of the need to adopt just another belief system. In the Kalama Sutta, the Buddha puts it like this:

> Don't be guided by reports, or tradition, or hearsay. Don't go by the authority of religious texts, nor by mere logic or inference, nor by considering appearances, nor by delight in speculative opinions, or by the idea: this is our teacher. When you know for yourselves that these qualities are unskillful and unwholesome, and lead to harm and suffering, abandon them. When you know for yourselves that other qualities are skillful and wholesome, encourage them.

....

The Dakini Speaks

My friends, let's grow up.

Let's stop pretending we don't know the deal here.

Or if we truly haven't noticed, let's wake up and notice.

Look: Everything that can be lost, will be lost.

It's simple—how could we have missed it for so long?

Let's grieve our losses fully, like ripe human beings.

But please, let's not be so shocked by them.

Let's not act so betrayed,

As though life had broken her secret promise to us.

Impermanence is life's only promise to us,

And she keeps it with ruthless impeccability.

To a child she seems cruel, but she is only wild,

And her compassion exquisitely precise:

Brilliantly penetrating, luminous with truth,

She strips away the unreal to show us the real.

This is the true ride—let's give ourselves to it!

Let's stop making deals for a safe passage:

There isn't one anyway, and the cost is too high.

We are not children anymore.

The true human adult gives everything for what cannot

be lost.

Let's dance the wild dance of no hope!

—Jennifer Welwood

....

For example, in Buddhist circles there can be endless discussions regarding the belief in past and future lives. People actually argue about such things, some scholars finding it essential that this teaching not be lost and others disdaining it as superstitious and not in keeping with what they consider to be the Buddha's greater wisdom. Another approach is to hold this question lightly and without arrogance, given that none of us can really know.

I wrote earlier about my parents frequently dropping me off at libraries. I was free to roam and read anything I desired. At one point when I was eleven, I picked up a book on rebirth. As I read it, I thought to myself: *This explains everything!* Whatever your relationship is to this question, however, it does seem to me to be truly limiting to have a solid concept of lives to come. I am sometimes part of conversations during which practitioners discuss what they want their next life to be. In the course of these conversations, I try to gently suggest that it may be wise to investigate their desires now instead of solidifying an imaginary future. Although the conversation appears to be about a life to come, it is really pointing to our state of mind. We need to have confidence in the fact that liberation is possible in the life we are living.

A deeper and more useful understanding of rebirth, put forward eloquently by the late Thai forest master Buddhadasa and others, is that we are reborn each moment. So the question is: How will we use this new life? That is, how will we practice in this moment now? If this is our vital question, our interest in a personal sense of continuous substantial absolute selfhood that has lived in the past and will continue into the future becomes less interesting. The question about rebirth dissolves as an issue to be pondered and resolved. In other words, we neither believe nor reject it, and our energy is freed to be directed into the practice.

What or who do we want to "hand our hearts over" to? When we put our hope into wanting particular situations or relationships, or our bodies to be a certain way, we may be shocked when things turn out to be otherwise. This shock happens on the level of the nervous system, beyond our conscious control. We feel betrayed at times by events that are out of our control. We feel betrayed by people we have put our trust in. We feel betrayed by our bodies and by life itself. It is essential not to judge ourselves when in the midst of shock. When the shock begins to ease, we can begin to examine the beliefs and assumptions we have held most dear. We can begin to investigate whether those beliefs and assumptions are true.

There is a wise and touching story about a woman named Kisagotami who lived in the time of the Buddha. When her son died, she felt utterly betrayed by life and, in her great grief, convinced herself that her son was just sick, rather than dead. Because anguish had affected her mind so profoundly, she hoped that perhaps her son just needed the right medicine to come back to life. After asking various people for help, someone eventually guided her to the Buddha. The Buddha said that he could help her, but that she needed to bring him some mustard seeds from a house in which no person had ever died. She set off on this mission with great zeal, assuming that bringing the Buddha some mustard seeds would be very easy.

She knocked on the door of the first house she saw, asked for some mustard seeds, and the man who answered happily gave her some. After accepting the seeds, she asked the second question, which is whether anyone in that house had died. The man said, yes, of course, someone in that house had died some time ago. So she went on to her second house to ask the same questions. The woman who answered the door in the second house replied in the same way. At house after house after house, the reply was the same: either someone in the house had recently died or someone had died long ago. She could not find one house in which no one had ever died.

Kisagotami began to understand that not only was she stricken by the death of a loved one, but that everyone is, at one time or another. She began her journey with the futile hope that her son could be saved, and as she did what the Buddha asked, her understanding shifted. She saw for herself that we are all in this together, that loss is nature. And because of this understanding, she was able to find peace in the worst of circumstances and to shift out of hope and into faith.

It is not that events or people or our bodies betray us. Rather, conditioned phenomenon always does what it does, which is to act according to its temporary and insubstantial nature. Accepting things as they are allows us to keep our hearts open in the midst of the pain. It's important to remember that this is a process. Acceptance is not always immediately and equally accessible at all times. Inner responsiveness to our own pain, instead of attributing our pain to another, offers a path to the joy, peace, and happiness that can be found within our own hearts. Without this orientation, we simply try to substitute one condition for another without pausing to check whether it is wise to do so. When our trust is challenged, a delicate investigation needs to occur. Blind belief without wisdom does not serve. There need to be grounds for trust and faith, based on our own experiences through the years. In difficult situations, our vision is easily clouded because past experiences of being let down are easily triggered. An early history of mistrust, perhaps having nothing to do with the details of a current situation, can have an undue impact on the present.

....

Some say you're lucky
If nothing shatters it.

But then you wouldn't
Understand poems or songs.
You'd never know
Beauty comes from loss.

It's deep inside every person:
A tear tinier
Than a pearl or thorn.

It's one of the places
Where the beloved is born.

—*Gregory Orr*

....

What are we handing our hearts over to? Treasuring the conditions we encounter, without dismissing them and dwelling in indifference, is treasuring our lives in the very midst of impermanence. At the same time, we have less and less unwarranted confidence in conditions being as we want them to be, because we know their temporary nature. We treasure conditions without clinging, in the here and now, and don't imagine any condition continuing into the future.

What comes in the wake of such trust is calm. We are calmer in the midst of the difficult. We are also able to summon courage when needed, and we develop the capacity to allow and accept. We are more apt to be able to act in wise and compassionate ways instead of panicking. What happens in the wake of trust is a sense of workability. We cannot know what will happen next. We will never know what will happen next. It is hard to live with the awareness that we don't know so sometimes we pretend this isn't so; we pretend that we do and can know. But as our practice matures, this idea dissipates and is replaced by the sense that everything is workable. This is where the practice takes us. Nothing is static. We grow in the confidence that come what may, we can meet the conditions presented.

....

Geese appear high over us,

pass, and the sky closes. Abandon,

as in love or sleep, holds

them to their way, clear

in the ancient faith: what we need

is here. And we pray, not

for new earth or heaven, but to be

quiet in heart, and in eye

clear. What we need is here.

—*Wendell Berry*

....

We live, based on the illusion of possible safety, in the midst of unpredictable conditions, somehow able to forget that there is no lasting safety in the temporary. Of course, in our culture there is a false reassurance regarding safety because the economy would fall apart if we didn't keep buying what we don't need. We hear messages all around us, encouraging us to try to buy our safety. We know this. I am not saying what each of us does not already know. But to know on ever deeper levels verifies this truth and also allows us to take the next step and to enter into groundlessness.

Groundlessness is a mere concept until we embody it. When embodied, we see clearly that everything really does change and that there is freedom in this understanding. As the poet Jennifer Welwood reminds us, "The true human adult gives everything for that which cannot be lost." We mature from hope into the confidence in groundlessness. Instead of trying to hold things together, we practice releasing and relinquishing, and we fall into joy.

One of the images that conveys groundlessness is of a person who falls off of a very high cliff. This person is in free fall, without anything to catch them. Terrified, the body tenses up. The mind is consumed with fear: "This is not going to end well!" However, after falling for some time, this person looks down and realizes that there is no ground. There is just empty space below. At this point, they relax. They begin to enjoy the falling. This person recognizes that they are being held by the Dharma, the nature of things, the way things are.

Clear seeing can only happen here and now. Our practice is to be present, to turn toward the here and now, to attend with love, and to relax. Patrul Rinpoche, a great Tibetan master, said, "Don't prolong the past. Don't invite the future. Don't be deceived by appearances. Just dwell in present awareness."

Instead of trying for a false security that takes great energy to convince ourselves of, can we be curious and interested instead? In turning toward the here and now with interest and affection, we discover a different kind of safety than can be found within conditions. We discover a refuge that no one and nothing can take away from us. This refuge is hard-won. And our hope shifts naturally into unshakable faith, the willingness to stay awake and to learn from all of our experiences.

PART IV

Liberation

12

Relaxing the Grasping

SOME YEARS AGO, A FRIEND sent me a video that was designed to teach babies and toddlers how to save themselves if they fall into a pool of water and no adult is around. The idea was to show them how to not panic and to float on their backs and relax until a grownup came to rescue them. My mother would have enjoyed this video. She often recalled having to get wet whether she wanted to or not every time she brought me to the beach because I would run headlong into the water and she would have to run in after me to keep me safe.

The beginning of the video frightened me because it shows a toddler running straight for the pool. No adult appears until later. The little boy runs straight for the pool, stumbles, and falls in. He begins to cry, but in the very same moment as he is crying, he does what he has been taught. He turns onto his back and floats, and of course, the water holds him up. Eventually an adult enters the pool—those watching the video can breathe again—and retrieves him. All is well.

....

First Lesson

Lie back, daughter, let your head

be tipped back in the cup of my hand.

Gently, and I will hold you. Spread

your arms wide, lie out on the stream

and look high at the gulls. A dead-

man's float is face down. You will dive

and swim soon enough where this tidewater

ebbs to the sea. Daughter, believe

me, when you tire on the long thrash

to your island, lie up, and survive.

As you float now, where I held you

and let go, remember when fear

cramps your heart what I told you:

lie gently and wide to the light-year

stars, lie back, and the sea will hold you.

—*Philip Booth*

....

Just as this small child has learned to let go and relax in the water of the pool, we too are in the process of learning to let go and relax into the still waters of the Dharma. Seeing things as they are, and accepting that they are the way they are, supports and holds us. One of the fruits of a dedicated practice is that in times of difficulty, the Dharma rises up to meet us.

My father was an elementary school teacher for most of his life, and he loved getting out of the classroom and taking the kids on field trips. He also taught swimming in the summer and worked as a lifeguard well into his eighties, finally retiring at the age of eighty-seven. In his upper eighties, he fell asleep from time to time while on the lifeguard stand. But the YMCA where he worked paired him with another lifeguard, one who could stay awake, and my father offered his services when he could. He was so delighted to receive a paycheck each week.

During his time at work, he was intent on making sure kids didn't run or engage in horseplay when close to the water. This meant he didn't have to jump in and save anyone very often. I think he saw it as preventative lifeguarding. In a similar way, Dharma practice can be understood as a form of preventative wisdom. We practice so that we can meet the conditions in life with greater grace, rather than drowning in their midst.

The Buddha said, "All that is subject to arising is subject to ceasing," and because of this fact, "nothing whatsoever should be clung to." The very nature of situations, conditions, phenomena, circumstances, people, things, and objects (all the same thing) is to change. This is the great law of impermanence. It naturally follows that letting go and living in an openhanded way is the only intelligent way to live. Doing so is actually our only option, other than to suffer.

And yet, we are deeply conditioned to grasp. It is not easy to let go. In the 1980s, Nancy Reagan tried to make letting go sound easy in relationship to drugs. She suggested people "Just Say No." And, of course, letting go, especially of addictions, is neither easy nor as simple as this. We want to let go, and at the same time, we want what we want.

As practitioners, we are on a path of gradual trust: trust in the path, trust in the practice, trust in ourselves, and trust in the laws of nature. We cannot let go of much of anything until we have enough trust and confidence that we will be held. It is not reasonable to think we can let go of anything without something else being put into place. This is where practice comes in. In the faith and trust that emerge gradually out of a dedicated meditation practice, letting go happens naturally, like a tree in fall lets go of its leaves.

It is tempting to try to force ourselves to let go, once we understand its necessity, but it is actually a delicate art rather than a matter of willpower. For example, when in a relationship that we know is unhealthy, we may think to ourselves, "I should let go." But telling ourselves what we *should* do is not fruitful and does not accomplish what we want. Letting go requires learning about our attachments so that we can see for ourselves that attachment does not bring the peace and happiness we are seeking.

The practice invites us to see and to study the limitations of attachment, to investigate whether it is possible to observe the suffering that is intertwined with the grasping. Undertaking a serious study of attachment and becoming intimate with grasping during ordinary moments in a day—as well as in times of great longing and overt loss—are the path to understanding that attachment is suffering. Sheer willpower can, of course, be useful at times, but it is limited. It is far different than wisdom. We need to be willing to see and to learn, rather than depending on willpower. Seeing attachments clearly and understanding that attaching does not bring peace allow for letting go.

The very words *letting go* can be problematic because they can sound as if we need to push away or get rid of something. Letting go can imply an overly active approach, motivated by an aversive mental state. *Letting be* is more accurate. Letting be does not rely on will-power. Rather, it is the willingness to inquire into, while opening to relaxation, ease, and spaciousness. It is like opening a fist. Instead of tensing up, we soften. Letting be is a natural process. Relaxing into the Dharma is relaxing into nature.

Attachment melts through awareness and patience and a growing understanding that grasping doesn't work in the way we hope it will. So often, we unconsciously hope that our grasping will be successful— at least this one time—and so we hold on even harder to that which is already slipping out of our grasp. Because of fearing we will be left without what we need, we cling even more.

As our understanding grows, we recognize on ever deeper levels that clinging is a losing proposition. But even when we know, we still cannot just let go, because genuine letting go is not a matter of will-power. We cannot force ourselves to let go. We have to experience attachment as it is. We have to get to know attachment to be able to see it as it is. As we do, it withers on its own. Attachment relaxes itself. What we are attached to will let go of us. What we can do is meet all phenomena with the wisdom of nongrasping.

This wisdom includes the understanding that we live our lives based on a fundamental error: the mistaken belief that happiness comes from temporary conditions and we don't have what we need within. We mistakenly believe that lasting peace and fulfillment can be found in an experience, person, situation, or object. We hope we will find what we need through a role as partner or parent, or through an identity related to job or career, or through our habits and views and opinions.

The main thing to be aware of is that attachment doesn't stand on its own. It is always in relationship to something. The problem is that if we over-focus on that something we are likely to overlook the underlying pattern of attachment. If we don't attend to the pattern, the objects of attachment will continue to change throughout our lives and our hearts will remain the same: empty and aching.

Letting go is a process. Most of the time, we are accompanied by a variety of emotions. The specificity of the emotions may vary according to differences in cultural experiences, family background, and gender conditioning, but it is natural for emotions to be part of the process.

I traveled to Taiwan in 2009 to see Master Sheng Yen, and he died a few days after I arrived. He had been very sick, so he had prepared for his death. As part of this preparation he had made a video to help his students remain peaceful while absorbing the fact of his absence. In this video, he talks about his own teacher's death. He speaks about the humanness of grief, as well as the naturalness of loss. It was a great help to many of us present.

When we cling, it is not possible to touch the essence of life. We cling because of the fear of emptiness, despair, and meaninglessness. We hold tightly to the known because of fearing the unknown. Even if the known is not what we want, it may feel more secure to try to hold on to what we know. This clinging keeps us bound to the contents of life—circumstances, relationships, and experiences—instead of opening the heart to life itself.

A key avenue of study is to recognize that attachment is strengthened through dwelling on whatever we are attached to. Dwelling, ruminating, and returning repeatedly to the object of attachment— its presence or absence—is the recipe for strengthening the attachment. We must ask ourselves: Where does our attention enjoy dwelling? Where do our minds go when we are not present? What takes us away from the here and now? What do we think about repeatedly? The answers point to our attachments.

It is possible for our attention to dwell anywhere. From the viewpoint of practice, we want to know what we are dwelling upon, because knowing is how we can see what we are attached to. Instead of having just a vague impression of attachments, it is clarifying to know exactly what we are attached to. What we are attached to need not be judged. In fact, it is essential to not judge. Judging muddies the waters and prevents us from clearly discerning love from attachment. If we judge what we are attached to, that judgment turns to blame. We will blame ourselves for our attachments or we will blame the objects of our attachments. Neither leads to peacefulness and letting go.

Nonattachment in relationships is not indifference or apathy. On the contrary we appreciate others more when we are not controlled by our attachment. We see one another for who we are. Otherwise, when attached, we try to make each other into how we want that person to be, in service to our personal agendas. It does not always look to us like self-centeredness, but it is: we are trying to make that person conform to our needs rather than respecting that their needs may be different than our own. Attachment is the effort to control; love is a greater sense of connectedness. Practice brings more love and less attachment. We learn to shift out of the habit of control and into the intention to connect.

As we practice diligently, we see our attachments gradually ebbing away, perhaps down to even just one attachment. Radical as it is, the practice is about letting go of all clinging entirely. In my course of teaching, I've noticed people see most of their attachments fall away, yet often one deeply cherished attachment remains. Because whatever we cling to is impermanent, that one attachment will still cause suffering. Nature is relentless in its teaching. We can bargain and negotiate all we want, and we will still suffer because what we are attached to is as impermanent as everything in this life.

When we are attached to anything, the world narrows. In our minds, we tend to isolate and over-focus on the one thing we have to have or not have, and in that process, we lose perspective. We leave everything else in life out and lose sight of the totality, cutting off a life of inner richness. Inner richness is accessed by openness and receptivity to what is happening now, instead of dwelling on repetitive themes.

In our study of our own attachment, being aware of a sense of urgency about anything is worth noting. Urgency is the inner pressure of having to own, to be, or to do. It is the burning need to get a desire met. When desire is strong enough, attaining the object of our desire seems absolutely necessary. Urgent clinging or desperate grasping is attachment and thus is suffering.

Grasping is distinct from simple wanting; simple wanting is not a problem. A creative and generous heart wants happiness for ourselves and others. It is wholesome to want such beneficial conditions as healthy bodies, connected relationships, and satisfying work; to incline toward well-being. This is not to be confused with efforts to force things to conform to our desires. Desires are held within the understanding that conditions are uncertain. We do our best to contribute to our own well-being and that of others. The error is in wanting to control the uncontrollable.

Nonattachment is not disconnection, indifference, withdrawal, or a negating of aspirations. What creates suffering is the urgency to control conditions that cannot be controlled.

Attachment implies a desire to control. As such, attachment to control also plays out in formal meditation in the effort to control the body/mind process. As we practice, we are learning the difference between training the mind and believing we have control over what arises in the mind.

Attachment can also be recognized in the form of anxiety. If we can approach the mind state of anxiety without aversion, and with curiosity, awareness of anxiety can lead to a deeper understanding. Awareness of anxiety reveals the belief that it can offer accurate information. It is beneficial to form the intention to avoid acting when anxiety is happening, because thoughts of anxiety cannot be depended upon. Anxiety manifesting as a thought is also a thought, and the thought does not need to be believed.

We practice shifting out of impulsivity and into intentionality, recognizing that impulse is based on habit. It is helpful to see how attachment fuels mental states. When we remember that events are out of our control—other people's behavior, circumstances, situations—we naturally let go of a control we do not possess anyway. The unawareness of anxiety creates a lack of confidence. The paradox of recognizing our lack of control is that trust and confidence are actually strengthened, because we are seeing the truth of things. Letting go then happens naturally.

....

There is no controlling life.

Try corralling a lightning bolt,

containing a tornado. Dam a

stream and it will create a new

channel. Resist, and the tide

will sweep you off your feet.

Allow, and grace will carry

you to higher ground. The only

safety lies in letting it all in—

the wild with the weak; fear,

fantasies, failures and success.

When loss rips off the doors of

the heart, or sadness veils your

vision with despair, practice

becomes simply bearing the truth.

In the choice to let go of your

known way of being, the whole

world is revealed to your new eyes.

—*Danna Faulds*

....

Working with attachment as a practice calls upon us to turn the attention away from what appears essential to our happiness. We drop the story about what is happening and turn the attention within. Reminding ourselves that we have what we need within, we experience what is "as it is." When attached, we lose our equilibrium; when we let go of attachment, we can recover our balance. We are in service to an agenda of self-comfort that does not even benefit ourselves. True ease can only be found by discovering our intrinsic peaceful nature.

Look closely: How does attachment manifest itself? What does it look like, what does it feel like in the body? What is the Dharma medicine? There are three different ways of approaching and working with attachment dependent on the form the attachment takes, three distinct kinds of medicine in response to each expression of attachment.

One form of attachment is the effort to sustain pleasure, to hold on to it, to make it last or last longer. This kind of attachment includes a sense of urgency. We want to own and possess. The Dharma medicine for this type of attachment is to practice nondwelling, ease, and spaciousness. While aware of what we are attached to, we practice including other elements of present moment experience as well. When we are trying to hold on to something, we tend to isolate it as something special. When we see something as special, we cling even more. The Dharma medicine is to minimize the tendency to isolate and to perceive what we are attached to as more important than whatever else is happening in life in this moment. In this regard, a wise question to ask is: What else is happening right now?

Attachment also appears in the form of rejection and judging. When an experience is unpleasant, our instinct is to try to push it away and get rid of it and to dwell in resistance and aversion. This is natural, but it does not alleviate suffering. Trying to push away what we don't like is a tried and untrue way to keep what we want to get rid of from leaving on its own. The effort keeps it locked in instead of allowing it to dissipate. Whatever we resist, will, due to that resistance, continue. The medicine in this case is the practice of acceptance and nonresistance. It is the practice of *allowing*. A wise question to ask in the midst of resistance and aversion is: Can I make space for this?

The third form of attachment is identification with something as being essential to who or what we are. This kind of attachment means seeing what is really just another impermanent element of life as inherently me, as who I am, instead of simply as another conditioned phenomena. The Dharma medicine is to see that all elements of life are nature, rather than self. What we experience is always just an experience. It is never who we are. This is universal and true for all beings.

In the stages of practice, we are instructed to find an anchor to steady the mind upon. This initial training helps us understand how not to cling to thinking. As we develop in steadiness and skillfulness, we can apply attentiveness to all phenomena. With metta and compassion as companions and allies, we gently allow the inner knots to untie themselves.

We cannot force letting go. However, we can practice allowing, acceptance, and nondwelling. We can study our attachments. We can inquire into the very nature of attachment. We can encourage ease and spaciousness. And we can view what is happening as nature and not-self.

Observing attachments even when subtle is imperative. We study attachment whether strong or weak. When our attachments are weak, we have a good chance to gather the strength to be able to see our stronger attachments. We can take an interest in how attachments manifest, in thoughts, emotions, speech, and actions. Following through, we can bring our attention to the results of attachment in daily situations in our lives. Does attachment really bring what the heart yearns for? Each of us needs to find this out for ourselves.

....

[She] saw that arising phenomena arose, abided, and passed away. She saw that the knowing of this arose, abided, and passed away. Then she knew there was nothing more than this, no ground, nothing to lean on stronger than the cane she held, nothing to lean upon at all and no one leaning and she opened the clenched fist in her mind and let go and fell into the midst of everything.

—*Sallie Teasdale, in* Women of the Way

....

We begin by accepting that we will attach, that we are wired to attach. This acceptance is part of the path, yet we don't stop with acceptance. We can also see that the practice offers an entirely different perspective than we have learned in the past, which allows for a natural deconditioning of the heart.

13

The Art of Questioning

THROUGHOUT THIS BOOK, I HAVE emphasized questioning as a way to practice. In this chapter, I will address the topic more deeply, pointing out a path leading to liberation that uses questioning as practice.

Not all questions are the same. Some ways of questioning are clarifying, while others mire us even more deeply in our conditioning. Asking wise questions and learning to lay aside the unwise ones is an important part of the art of meditative questioning.

There was a time, some forty or so years ago, when Cambridge, Massachusetts, where the Cambridge Insight Meditation Center is located, was a lively place for those interested in the spiritual life. Many teachers from many traditions regularly came into town. My friends and I would visit these different teachers to ask for guidance and to find out what they were teaching. These teachers would expound upon their teachings and would also sometimes criticize the teachings of others, either in their own tradition or a different one.

This reminded my friends and me of one of the discourses of the Buddha called the Kalama Sutta, which I referenced in an earlier chapter. In this sutta, the Buddha spoke about a variety of teachers who visited the town of Kalama. Each teacher offered contradictory teachings about the nature of suffering and happiness, leaving the residents of Kalama confused. Cambridge appeared, in some ways, similar to Kalama, and the Buddha's instructions to question rather than to simply adopt one more belief system was, for me, especially pertinent advice.

In the Buddhist tradition, questioning is greatly valued. The Buddha encouraged questioning as a way to a deeper understanding of suffering and liberation. He instructed his devotees not to blindly believe or accept a teaching simply because someone has told us to or because it is in the teachings.

We are encouraged to test the teachings out for ourselves, to experiment, and to rely on our direct experience. All of the teachings have only to do with suffering and the end of suffering. The Buddha did not want us to passively accept what he or anyone else said, but rather to find out for ourselves if a teaching is worthwhile and true and leads to liberation from suffering. If we find that it does, the Buddha suggested we apply it and live it. Faith in Buddhist practice is based on our own experience, not on blind acceptance. What verifiably reduces our suffering and the suffering of those around us? What compounds suffering and makes it worse?

The teachers I have been drawn to most on this path have emphasized investigation and questioning. One of these teachers was the great sage Krishnamurti, who used inquiry as a fundamental tool in his teaching. I first encountered a book of his when I was sixteen;

it affected me deeply. Another was Ajahn Maha Boowa, whom I've referred to throughout this book. He struck me as intensely investigative when I first met him, and my meetings with him verified this initial impression. Master Sheng Yen, with whom I practiced for over ten years, had one of the most alive outlooks and approaches to the deepest questions in life of anyone I have ever known. All three of these teachers shared the qualities of openness and curiosity.

One of the basic questions we might ask as meditators is this: Why am I not already awake if awakening is so important to me? Or, of equal importance: How do I practice in the midst of adversity? Questions such as these don't have conceptual answers. They are questions that point us toward answers emanating from the heart.

What is the foundation for fruitful questioning, so that our questions do not just reflect more conditioned thinking? The foundation for fruitful questioning is, ultimately, the development of inner steadiness. We need to have some degree of calm and tranquility to be able to investigate, but this is not, in itself, enough. It is like putting a Band-Aid on a wound. The bandage helps, of course, by protecting the wound from getting infected. But some wounds need, like deep suffering, more than a Band-Aid. Calm and steadiness are the same: essential and beneficial but not ultimately healing and freeing.

Meditative questioning is a method of investigation. We do need enough calm to be able to look into agitation instead of simply being caught in it. We need enough happiness to be capable of looking into unhappiness. Otherwise we will just be lost in unhappiness. We need enough steadiness to be able to fruitfully look into fragility and unpredictability, and we need enough stability to be able to look into impermanence, loss, and change, without being caught in despair.

A foundation of peace allows us to investigate our most meaningful questions, without cycling around in thought after thought—which of course we are very good at doing without any practice or instruction whatsoever.

Asking a wise question enlivens the practice in a way that nothing else can. Wise and meditative questions are ways to look into and drop our assumptions, preconceptions, and unexamined beliefs. Our intention when we question in this way is to learn, not simply to accumulate knowledge but to encourage relaxation so that we can receive a deeper wisdom.

One important component of the art of questioning is distinguishing between questions that are useful and those that are not. If we pay close attention to our minds, we may well notice that we are actually always asking questions, although a lot of the time we are not doing so consciously and a lot of the questions are not useful. When in sitting meditation, we ask questions such as how long has the sitting lasted so far and when will it end? Has the teacher leading the sitting fallen asleep? Do I need to run up front and save my fellow meditators by ringing the bell? Well, maybe it doesn't get quite that dramatic, but these are examples of questions that we are not always conscious of asking and that do not lead anywhere.

The four kinds of questions I will reflect upon are those concerning doubt, questions not worth asking, life questions, and meditative questions. It is important to distinguish among these four types. The first two we need to recognize and let go of, and the third and fourth we need to ask often and then drop the tendency to want to know the answer, instead listening inwardly with interest and spaciousness.

Questions having to do with doubt are easy to miss because they seem so believable. Such questions appear to be utterly reasonable and valid, and yet all they ever do is simply perpetuate more doubt. Instead of settling and grounding, we find ourselves spinning from one doubt thought to the next, hoping our thoughts will figure the whole thing out for us. This will never happen. Thinking will not take us to inner freedom.

One common question about doubt is: Is this the best place to be? The reality is that wherever we are is the best place to be because it is where we are. I am not referring to dangerous situations, of course, which we need to respond to appropriately. I am referring to those many moments when our minds are spinning around, telling us that there is a better place to be than where we are. Yet the body is where it is. A meditative response to this question is to unify the mind with the body by bringing the mind into the body, instead of dreaming about being in a better place.

There always seems to be a better place to be or something else to do that may be more enjoyable or meaningful. Of course, we need to look at our lives to see if we are living wisely. But the pull to be somewhere we are not can be quite strong, and social media can reinforce this mind state. Some studies find that people feel more depressed if they spend a lot of time on social media. Some forms of social media such as Facebook can foster the fear of missing out, of thinking others are far happier than we are. Meditators, of course, often connect to the joy of missing out, recognizing the quiet pleasures in life. The contemplative's ancient echo is that here is where peace is to be found.

Another question having to do with doubt is the question of whether the method of practice we are engaged in is the best one. In the United States, there are many practices to choose from. We read one Dharma book that tells us one thing, only to be contradicted by another book telling us the opposite thing. Contradictions can even be found in the very same tradition. How can we assess these differences? The Buddha said that if a system leads to clinging and unwholesome mental states, let it go. If it leads to relinquishment, love, and wisdom, we know it is worthwhile.

The object of meditation, such as the breath, is not as important as the awareness of the object. When I first began to meditate, the instructions were to be aware of the breathing. This was difficult for me. Because I had practiced *pranayama* (regulated breathing practiced in yoga traditions) for some years before being introduced to meditation, I couldn't help but control my breath, instead of just letting the breath breathe itself. For some years, I felt I was doing something wrong by being aware of sound or of the whole body just sitting. Only when I gained some confidence in my own capacity to know what was right for me did the practice become enjoyable.

Self-doubt, the suspicion that we are not capable of meditating and that we are always doing it wrong, is daunting. Many of us are deeply conditioned to doubt ourselves in all arenas of life. It is unrealistic to think we won't experience doubt as we meditate, simply because of its presence everywhere else. Doubt that we are not able to practice is, in the end, just doubt. Questioning our capacity to practice can easily derail our aspirations.

Questions having to do with doubt are not unimportant, but trying to answer them on our own is not likely to be fruitful. It is like conditioning trying to answer its own conditioning. A skillful response is to expose these kinds of questions to the light by asking questions of those we trust such as teachers and friends. Don't invest your energy in the effort to answer yourself. Recognize thoughts that have doubt as their theme as thoughts, and try not to get caught up in them.

The second kind of question that is not fruitful to consider is what I call *wrong questions*. These are questions that are not worth asking at all, questions to be put aside entirely. Wrong questions reinforce conditioning instead of dissolving it, leading to greater confusion and agitation instead of to more clarity and peace.

As I discussed in the chapter on painful emotions, the question of *why* a particular experience is occurring is the wrong question to ask from a meditative point of view. If we lay this question aside without ruminating on it, we might notice that we only ask this question when an experience is unpleasant. When an experience is pleasant, we might notice that we simply enjoy the experience without asking why it is occurring. By observing without trying to answer a "wrong" question, we can look more deeply and see that we just don't like unpleasant experiences, that we are relating to the unpleasant with aversion. We might also notice that what we are really asking is why a particular experience is happening "to me." Again, in not trying to answer the question of *why*, we can look more deeply and recognize that unpleasant experiences happen to everyone and are not personal.

If we don't relate to an inner experience as a problem, the question of *why* it is happening will not arise. We can see the cause in the here and now. When we relate to an experience as a problem, we also believe that that experience should not be happening. If an experience should not be happening, it follows that the question of why would automatically arise. But why should it not be happening? Isn't that just an opinion, given the actuality of our experience?

An example is the experience of sleepiness while sitting. From one point of view, the cause may be that we haven't slept well the night before. But the cause of *suffering*, here and now, is that we are not paying close enough attention. With the willingness to drop the question of *why* and pay closer attention to the actual experience, the sleepiness may remain, but we are able to see sleepiness as an object of meditation, instead of relating to it as a problem. When we view experiences in this way, wisdom can arise, instead of attempting to push experiences away. In dropping the question of *why*, we can ask the skillful question of *how*: How am I relating to what is happening here and now? Many of the questions we habitually ask about our experiences lead to greater confusion and agitation, rather than to relaxation and insight. These questions are simply habits of mind and are best put aside, rather than trying to find an answer.

The third category is life questions, questions that have to do with our lives as a whole. This means the fears, dreams, and confusions that bubble up repeatedly during different phases of a life. The changing conditions in a life bring forth different questions. These kinds of questions are of another order than the previous two and can be fruitful and deeply meaningful. Rather than being questions that we turn into problems, these are problems that we learn to turn into questions. These singular kinds of questions are akin to Zen koans; they are questions that cannot be answered through mere reasoning, but must be lived into. As a teacher, as I get to know a practitioner, I find one particular heartfelt question arising for that practitioner, time after time again, asked in different ways but always coming back to the same question.

Some examples of life questions are: What is my practice in the face of great adversity? When life is unjust, what is equanimity? Are other people ever to blame? Why be present when I can mentally escape my life? Is fear within me, or is there cause to be afraid? If I lost what is most precious to me, would I survive?

Life questions are precious; they are precious jewels in our lives. We need to respect our life questions and have great patience with them. Although there may not be an intellectual answer that satisfies, there can indeed be a resolution—an ending of confusion. In other words, whatever it is, the problem is no longer a problem. The issue simply dissolves.

It is important to understand that our relationship to issues and problems can change. The same situation may exist with all of the same particularities, but our relationship to it may change so profoundly that something that bothered us immensely in the past doesn't bother us at all anymore. The issue has resolved itself completely, not by being ignored or judged but through being held with loving awareness. All questions, even such a question as "What is the meaning of life?" are resolved, in that we no longer think about or experience angst in relationship to what was once an immense issue for us. The issue does not arise in the mind as one that needs to be thought about or pondered.

An unshakable faith can emerge when we learn to trust these kinds of questions. With the intention to face all of our experiences in life—especially the most confusing—with openheartedness and interest, our life questions dissolve rather than resolve. We might not be able to articulate what change has occurred, or when or how, but we are aware that we are no longer bothered in the way we once were.

Life dilemmas can be turned into questions, and how we live our lives becomes our answer. The ways we live and think and act and speak express our practice in a manner that no conceptual explanation can.

....

I would like to beg you to have patience with everything unresolved in your heart and try to love the questions themselves as if they were locked rooms or books written in a very foreign language. Don't search for the answers, which could not be given to you now, because you would not be able to live them. And the point is, to live everything. Live the questions now. Perhaps then, someday far in the future, you will gradually, without even noticing it, live your way into the answer.

—*Rainer Maria Rilke*

....

The last category is meditative questions. Meditative questions are always well worth asking. They are asked in the service of wisdom, of deepening our understanding, and of finding freedom from suffering. Meditative questions point beyond conditions and pertain to right now. They encourage an ongoing interest in looking below the surface appearance of things.

Like our life koans, meditative questions also cannot be answered solely by the intellect. The asking of a meditative question, in and of itself, awakens an innate wisdom. We ask the question and then let go of any mental answers that arise. To practice with such questions is to relinquish the desire for results, because the desire for an answer obscures true insight.

The practice of asking meditative questions is like throwing a stone in a pond. After throwing the stone, we observe and we listen. We don't throw stone after stone. Every now and then, we ask a question and then listen with great attentiveness and care. We don't focus on questions that bring restlessness and doubt. We also don't ask too many meditative questions; just one can do for several months at a time. Sometimes we stumble inadvertently upon a great question, finding one that captivates our attention and wakes us up. When that happens, use that one question until it wears itself out. The point of all this is to foster an attitude of openness and curiosity.

Each of us has different questions that matter to us. If you discover a good question, keep it alive, and ask it under all circumstances. The key is to ask it in all situations, not just some. A meditative question needs to be applied to all conditions if we are to see into things differently than we previously have.

One question I asked for more than a year was this: Can another moment be better than the moment I am in now? I asked it when experiences were fine, and I asked it in the midst of pain. I asked this question whenever I thought to ask it, as a practice throughout the day. When I began to ask, I knew the answer, but only intellectually, not through my lived experience. From an intellectual point of view, it's easy to know that there cannot be any better moment than the one we are in, because this is the only moment there is. But to know this and live it are quite different than believing it in theory.

An authentic meditative question is always fresh and distinct from a conditioned thought. It has the potential to take us to silence, ease, peace, and spaciousness. The difference between wise reflection and conditioned thinking is that in thinking, there is clinging and suffering. In reflection, there is curiosity and exploration.

Ask what you are genuinely interested in, not what you think you should be interested in. An inner sense grows as to which questions bring true peace and lead to more peace and which bring ever greater confusion. Meditative questions are ways to guide our lives and discover inner liberation.

In asking a meditative question, we develop a natural inclination toward investigation. As this growing interest in inquiry occurs, we use whatever questions naturally arise. Questioning in this way is liberating. The question itself is a bridge from the conditioned to the unconditioned, and thus from confusion to inner freedom.

Here are some possible meditative questions:

Who is it that is upset? Who is angry?

What is the mind aware of right now?

If I am not happy in this moment, why not?

When I experience emotional turbulence, what do I do?

When there is thinking—how does it affect sensations and emotions?

How do emotions affect thoughts?

Is this thought both true and useful?

Given the conditions in my life right now, what is wise effort?

How am I reacting to this experience?

Is it possible to approach this experience with wisdom and compassion?

What is the quality of my heart right now?
What does love free of attachment look like?

We ask such questions with innocence and curiosity, free from efforts to try to feel differently than we do. Our questioning is not an attempt to repress our feelings or to try to make ourselves cooperate with a Dharma viewpoint, nor is it going along with what someone says we should think. We don't ask a question while simultaneously trying to tell ourselves how we should feel or what we should be experiencing. We explore and open to different perspectives to see for ourselves what emerges.

In this way, liberation becomes possible.

....

Sometimes you hear a voice through the door
calling you, as fish out of water
hear the waves, or a hunting falcon
hears the drum's *Come back. Come back.*

This turning toward what you deeply love
saves you. Read the book of your life,
which has been given you.

A voice comes to your soul saying,
Lift your foot. Cross over.

Move into the emptiness
of question and answer and question.

—*Rumi*

....

....

Poem without a Category

Trailing my stick I go down to the garden edge,

call to a monk to go out the pine gate.

A cup of tea with my mother,

looking at each other, enjoying our tea together.

In the deep lanes, few people in sight;

the dog barks when anyone comes or goes.

Fall floods have washed away the planks of the bridge;

shouldering our sandals, we wade the narrow stream.

By the roadside, a small pavilion

where there used to be a little hill:

it helps out our hermit mood;

country poems pile one sheet on another.

I dabble in the flow, delighted by the shallowness of the stream,

gaze at the flagging, admiring how firm the stones are.

The point in life is to know what's enough—

why envy those otherworld immortals?

With the happiness held in one inch-square heart

you can fill the whole space between heaven and earth.

— Gensei, Japanese monk

....

14

Nirvana Is Enoughness

I BEGAN THIS BOOK BY REFLECTING ON LOSS.

One classical way the Buddha described coming to terms with loss is through reflecting on and taking to heart the five recollections. The five recollections help us to recognize and accept the realities in our lives—the fact that we are subject to old age, sickness, and death and will lose everything dear to us. The paradox is that in embracing these truths, another way of living is illuminated. The path is made visible as we walk it, and we begin to see for ourselves that the cause of dissatisfaction is grasping and attaching to that which is temporary, intrinsically insubstantial, and can provide only limited satisfaction. In seeing the true nature of phenomena, we turn toward buddha nature, which is an absence of attachment and a fullness of love, compassion, joy, and equanimity.

In the first chapter, I referred to Ajahn Maha Boowa's description of suffering as "a constant squeeze." I mention it here, again, to emphasize the fact that the start of the path is the recognition of suffering. We begin to turn toward this ache within the heart with compassionate attentiveness instead of seeking to avoid it. As Ajahn Chah said, there is the suffering that leads to further suffering and the suffering that leads to the end of suffering, to lasting peacefulness. To ignore the constant squeeze leads to greater sorrow. To turn toward the ache in the heart is painful and uncomfortable—and leads to its end.

Ajahn Maha Boowa defined the word *nirvana* as "enough." As we dedicate ourselves to the practice, the sense of feeling constantly squeezed by conditions in life begins to ease, and we discover an inner enoughness. As we well know, we can't ever have enough when it comes to the conditions in life. What Ajahn Maha Boowa is referring to is a dimension of being that is free from a sense of insufficiency.

What does *enough* mean? It means knowing an inner wholeness. Nirvana is complete; another definition of dukkha is "incompleteness." The dictionary definition of *enough* is used in reference to conditions. "Nirvana is enough" points toward the unconditioned, the now. In understanding the nature of phenomena—dropping our hopes and beliefs that any condition, object, circumstance, relationship, phenomena, or situation will ever be completely satisfying all of the time—we let go of clinging and discover an inner wholeness in which nothing is lacking.

We can, and we often do, find a temporary refuge in conditions. Perhaps we find refuge and beauty in the work that we do. We find connectedness and sustenance in inspiring relationships with intimate partners, family, and friends. Throughout each day, we meet conditions to be appreciated and delighted by. But none of these conditions are ultimately reliable; all will change and pass.

As I come to the end of this book, the conditions in my life are all I would desire. And yet, I know this set of conditions too will not last, because they *cannot* last. Knowing this, I can practice treasuring without clinging, loving without attaching, cherishing without grasping.

I don't mean to dismiss the conditions in our lives as if they don't matter. They do matter. And, at some times in life, enough takes on a different meaning than how I've been writing about it thus far. At times we must say: enough! We need to change conditions when conditions can be changed. Conditions can be beneficial or not and can help our practice or hinder it. Just because we will lose everything eventually does not mean we drop into complacency or indifference. Being a true practitioner means helping to alleviate pain in this world and being present for one another.

....

For a long time I wondered why I felt like bowing when people showed their appreciation for the work that I have been privileged to do. What I have come to understand is that we who bow are acknowledging the presence of the eternal: we're bowing to the eternal in our neighbor. In loving and appreciating our neighbor, we are participating in something truly sacred.

—Mr. (Fred) Rogers

....

Life involves choosing forms. It is worth noting that conditions are not interchangeable. The person we choose to be intimate with is not interchangeable with someone else, those we are friends with are people with whom we choose to be friends. We aspire to be friendly and kind to all beings, but true freedom does not include literally inviting "all beings" into our home. We have to choose forms. Choosing forms is part of this life. We choose forms, and we practice those forms. If we are in an intimate relationship, can this relationship be practice? If we are on our own, can being alone be practice? If we have chosen to ordain, can being ordained be practice?

We are not somehow a partial person if we don't have a companion. We are already whole within ourselves. Enoughness is always available. Instead of trying to get closer to others, the question is whether we can get closer to our own hearts and minds. As we do, we discover that we can share with one another in more intimate ways.

We often fear that something is missing within us, that something is wrong with us. We live with the pervasive sense that we are not enough, and no matter how much we try, we will never be enough. No matter how much we are praised, the praise is not enough. No matter how much we succeed in something important to us, our success is not enough. When we get something, we want more of it. We think: *If only I tried harder, I might get what I need, conditions might give me what I need.* But neither inner conditions—thoughts, sights, sounds, tastes, smells, touches, feelings—nor outer circumstances will ever be enough. We keep waiting for something to complete us.

This is "worldly waiting"—waiting for something better to happen in a moment in the future. There is also such a thing as "sacred waiting." Sacred waiting is a receptivity of heart. We are not waiting for some thing to occur that is not happening now. Rather, we are open to the sacred revealing itself in the here and now.

It is paradoxically true that something is indeed missing: the wisdom of knowing that nothing is missing. The truth is that we will never be enough if we continue down the path of trying to fill ourselves through getting and accumulating. We will only succeed in reifying the delusion that we are not enough. We live in a culture in which consumption reigns supreme, yet our inner culture can be one of letting go. Letting go is a true refuge.

When we feel a lack in any dimension in our lives, our instinct is to try to hold on to whatever little we have. Letting go is counterintuitive. And yet, letting go is not compromise or resignation. Letting go happens in relation to the degree of understanding we have of enoughness. To whatever degree we know that we deeply have what we need within ourselves, we will let go.

We gradually learn to trust that we have what we need. People talk about "getting enlightened," but it is more accurate to speak about letting go of delusion regarding our true nature. Our true nature is the same as the nature of the Buddha. It is no different.

Years ago, I met a Zen abbess, Shundo Aoyama, just before leaving for a three-month silent retreat. She was visiting Cambridge, and I was able to have tea with her. I decided to ask her for general advice about the retreat. I asked, "Do you have any advice for me to keep in mind during the next three months of silence?" She replied very simply: "Just come back more like yourself."

I remember feeling surprised and somewhat disconcerted by her response. I also felt somehow thwarted. My secret plan, which I hadn't confided to anyone, was to try to come back as *someone else*. I felt at that time that pretty much anyone else would do. I wasn't picky.

She was pointing out that I was enough, that I already had what I needed within. She was showing me that ideas of spiritual attainment were unnecessary and I only needed to be completely confident in my own buddha nature. She was not implying that I was particularly special or wonderful, so utterly wonderful that I did not need to be anyone else other than my own special self. She was teaching me that none of us needs to be anything other than aware of our buddha nature, which is the same as everyone else's buddha nature.

In the knowing of enough, we are at home within ourselves, wherever we are. We don't have to be with exactly the "right" person all the time, or in "perfect" circumstances. Inner spaciousness becomes available, and we are comfortable and at ease. Personal ambition drops away, yet our efforts in practice do not diminish.

As practitioners we tend to feel that our practice is not good enough. We compare ourselves with others and come up short. When we do so, the practice becomes a burden instead of a path of liberation. Instead of simply walking the path, it becomes "my" path, "my" practice, as if it were something we could own or possess. We turn our years of dedicated practice back onto ourselves and weigh ourselves down by our meditative histories. If we have been on this path for a significant period of time, we imagine we should be "farther along" than we think we are. But as our practice deepens, measuring and evaluating are what drop away. We no longer think of ourselves as terrible practitioners who have achieved nothing or as great practitioners who have achieved a lot. Assessing ourselves as better than, worse than, or equal to other practitioners dissolves. We recognize thoughts and feelings of comparison as thoughts of delusion, as moments of being lost in the illusion of separation.

The practice is to stay steady and not be swayed or seduced by the concocted stories we weave. We practice withdrawing our naive faith that our stories are true and we just need to try harder. Trying harder holds the belief that "I" need to try harder.

An ancient Zen master asks us, "What, in this moment, is lacking? If not now, when?" Right here and now: What is lacking? What is wrong? Is there any better moment than right now? When we initially ask this, the first answer that comes to mind is that there had better be. Let this answer pass away. With deep listening and patience, we see that there cannot be a better moment, that thoughts about the past are thoughts and not the past itself, and that thoughts about the future are imaginative. When we recognize this, we see that there is no better or worse moment than this one. Our understanding invites us to embrace the here and now of life as it is and encourages us to respond to the conditions we are facing with greater wisdom and compassion.

I mentioned my friend Sarah earlier, who lives in assisted living where there are many visible reminders and signs of death. She uses these reminders not just to accept the fact of death—which she sees as a lesser understanding—but as pointers to the here and now. She is aware of the absence of boredom; her interest in learning the deepest of meditative truths is unwavering. She is not concerned with how much longer she will live. She is focused on being present. Living in this way, she experiences great contentment in the smallest of things. A sip of coffee, the breeze on her skin—each moment awakens her. She reports that this stage in her life is the most exciting thus far. She is clearly cultivating contentment. Cultivating contentment is a practice. Instead of dwelling on the desire to be content, we have to keep letting go of the habit of clinging, to uncover this basic sense of wholeness and sanity. This wholeness is synonymous with enoughness.

When we are not in touch with enoughness, we are like hungry ghosts. In Buddhist cosmology, the concept of a hungry ghost implies a hunger that cannot be satisfied, a thirst that cannot be quenched. The image of the hungry ghost is of a being with a very large belly and a tiny mouth. So even though a person with hungry ghost mind is trying to nourish themselves, they can never eat quite enough to feel full. The hunger or thirst cannot be quenched because they are looking in the wrong place for satiation. The impoverishment is inner rather than outer. What a hungry ghost needs is nourishment for the heart, rather than food for the body.

Not only do we think we do not have enough, we also think we can never do enough. Instead of giving a wholehearted attentiveness to what we are doing now, we often act halfheartedly, reserving our full attention for an imaginary moment that may never come. When we lose ourselves in efforts to get something done, we also lose a sense of awe and mystery. We find ourselves lost in intensity instead of being appreciative of the ordinary. In the awareness of enough, how could there be anything other than a richness of gratitude and appreciation?

We have a wooden altar at the Cambridge Insight Meditation Center with beautiful carvings on it. The person teaching sits in front of it, facing the meditation hall. On the right side of the altar there is a bodhisattva holding a flower, and on the left, a bodhisattva holding a sword. The flower signifies compassion; the sword is the sword of wisdom, cutting through habits, patterns, and ignorance. When we become aware of our conditioned patterns of mind that are unworthy of our aspirations for freedom, we bring compassion to those patterns. We see the pain held in those patterns and the ways those patterns have functioned as efforts to protect us in the past. And we realize these patterns are impersonal and suffering. The sword of wisdom represents our capacity to cut through confusion and delusion. We touch the ground and bear witness with the same gesture that the Buddha used when being faced with his own inner conditioning.

We can take up enoughness as a practice. Is right now enough? Again, the practice of meditation is not one oriented toward self-improvement. In fact, the practice shows us that what we call "myself" is a process rather than an object that needs to be fixed. Enoughness shifts our perspective. Instead of thinking of a day or a life as something to be used, can we allow life to use us? Can this moment simply be appreciated?

Another word for "enough" is *whole*. We can live our entire lives sensing that there is a hole within us and trying to fill that hole in countless ways. If we don't question this way of living, we will always feel deprived and lacking in what we are and need. We will be lost in insecurity and anxiety and caught in doubt, confusion, and fear. In other words, we will suffer. In awareness of enough, fear and anxiety drop away.

Before beginning to practice, I tried to fill that hole in every way I could find. I was quite creative, but basically just found new ways to suffer. Because of this creativity and dedication to filling that hole, I experienced exhaustion and disenchantment early in my life. Finally, I had the great fortune to discover the Buddha's teachings and practice instructions. I was ready, and if you are reading a book like this, you are too.

The point of the practice is to train the mind to discover the deathless, the sacred, enough. Let us keep practicing together with great dedication until we all know this for ourselves.

....

Searching for spring all day, I never saw it,
straw sandals treading everywhere
among the clouds, along the bank.

Coming home, I laughed, catching
the plum blossom's scent:
Spring at each branch tip, already perfect.

—*anonymous nun, Sung dynasty China*

....

Credits

"Sonnets to Orpheus, 11, 13" from *Selected Poetry of Ranier Maria Rilke* by Rainer Maria Rilke, translated by Stephen Mitchell, translation copyright (that little copyright symbol) 1080, 1981, 1982 by Stephen Mitchell. Used by permission of Random House, an imprint and division of Penguin Random House LLC. All rights reserved.

"Magnanimous Heart is like a mountain" by K. Uchiyama, *From the Zen Kitchen to Enlightenment,* translated by Thomas Wright. New York: Weatherhill, 1983.

"A Cedary Fragrance" from *Given Sugar, Given Salt* by Jane Hirshfield. Copyright © 2001 by Jane Hirshfield. Reprinted by permission of HarperCollins Publishers.

"If your mind becomes firm like a rock" from *The Buddha Speaks,* edited by Anne Bancroft. ©2000 by Anne Bancroft. Reprinted by

Index

About the Author

NARAYAN HELEN LIEBENSON is a guiding teacher at the Cambridge Insight Meditation Center in Cambridge, Massachusetts, and has been teaching there since its inception in 1985. Narayan is also a guiding teacher at the Insight Meditation Society in Barre, Massachusetts, where she offers residential retreats. She leads retreats as well in other parts of the country and the world.

Her training over the past forty years includes study in the United States and in Asia with meditation masters in the Theravada, Zen, and Tibetan traditions. She was a student of the late Chan master Sheng Yen for over ten years. Asked by Master Sheng Yen to teach, Narayan decided to integrate her understanding of Zen into her already existing Vipassana lineage.

Narayan is the author and illustrator of a small book titled *Life as Meditation*, and for many years wrote a meditator's advice column in *Buddhadharma* magazine.

What to Read Next
from Wisdom Publications

A Buddhist Grief Observed
Guy Newland

"Guy Newland's *A Buddhist Grief Observed* is a powerful reflection on his experience of losing his wife to cancer . . . an extraordinary book."—*Buddhadharma*

Emptiness
A Practical Guide for Meditators
Guy Armstrong

"For anyone seeking to understand emptiness, this is a clear and fine guidebook, with precise and practical ways to explore and deepen your practice."—Jack Kornfield, author of *A Path With Heart*

Bearing the Unbearable
Love, Loss, and the Heartbreaking Path of Grief
Joanne Cacciatore
Foreword by Jeffrey Rubin

"Simultaneously heartwrenching and uplifting. Cacciatore offers practical guidance on coping with profound and life-changing grief. This book is destined to be a classic . . . [it] is simply the best book I have ever read on the process of grief."—Ira Israel, *The Huffington Post*

About Wisdom Publications

Wisdom Publications is the leading publisher of classic and contemporary Buddhist books and practical works on mindfulness. To learn more about us or to explore our other books, please visit our website at wisdompubs.org or contact us at the address below.

Wisdom Publications
199 Elm Street
Somerville, MA 02144 USA

We are a 501(c)(3) organization, and donations in support of our mission are tax deductible.

Wisdom Publications is affiliated with the Foundation for the Preservation of the Mahayana Tradition (FPMT).